A NEED
FOR
Nigel

THE TRUE STORY

CAMIKA SHELBY

ISBN: 979-8-9884486-4-8

Publishing By:
DemiCo National, LLC
www.DemiCoNational.com

Editor: Miah Alexander

Dedication

In loving memory of Nigel Ahmad Shelby, and as a tribute to all the parents who have endured the loss of their children to suicide. To the resilient LGBTQ Community, facing the struggle for acceptance while confronting the challenges of mental health, this book is dedicated to your strength and perseverance.

TABLE OF CONTENTS

PROLOGUE

Growing up in Lincoln projects in Huntsville, Alabama—some call it "LP," the hood, the ghetto, the PJ's or any other terminology that one would use to undermine low-class black people. Whichever way you decide to put it, it was LOVE and sometimes dysfunctional. In our culture, there are family secrets and abuse that are swept under the rug. No one truly knows their identity because they're used to being told who, what, and how to be someone they're not. The slave mentality. That was never me though, I always felt the need to march to the beat of my own drum.

Of course, that's the Leo in me–dominant, assertive, stubborn, aggressive, and totally confident in who I am at times. However, there are times where I feel timid, insecure, and unsure of myself, but those moments don't last long. Somehow, I always tend to come back.

Never in a million years would I think that I'd be sitting in front of a therapist airing all of my thoughts, demons, breakdowns, happy moments, and here we are—the worst nightmare that I have had to live through thus far.

Dr. Zee spoke. "Ms. Shelby, tell me about the day of April 18, 2019." My heart felt as if it stopped beating as I parted my lips to speak back to Dr. Zee. With my eyes closed and unconsciously rolling, I said, "It's 3 o'clock in the morning, and my eyes were popped open by the sound of my phone's alarm, "SHIT, another day of this bull shit!" But of course, another day, another dollar. I silenced my alarm and reached over to the nightstand to turn on the lamp. As my feet hit the cold floor, a sudden chill rushed through my body. I proceeded to make up my bed as I normally would every morning, then headed to the bathroom to shower and brush my teeth. For some reason, it took me a while to leave the bathroom mirror. I stared at myself for an extended period of time—longer than usual. Shake it off Mika, I thought to myself.

Finally dressed for work, I left the bathroom and stuck my head into my son's bedroom. There he was lying in his bed sleeping peacefully—that alone put the brightest smile on my face. As I'm sitting in my therapist's office, with my face in my hand, anxiety thrusting through my body like never before; my thoughts start to reverse back to the very beginning. The day that I gave life to a beautiful and unique soul. My son. My one and only child. My Nigel.

MOST PRAISED CHAMPION

Keta, Keta, Keta, I yelled repeatedly as I watched water run down my leg, onto the floor. She runs in and yells, "What's wrong?" I looked her in the eyes and said, "It's time–my water just broke."

She responded, "Ok, stay calm and slowly get up." My bags were already packed for my hospital stay so Keta grabbed them along with my car keys as we were headed out the door. Flying down Interstate 565, hazard lights flashing, and me of course–anxious as ever, clenching the front passenger's seat belt, thinking, "I'm finally about to become a mother." The doctors told me that I wouldn't ever have children, and I have already had two miscarriages. BUT here we are with a full-term pregnancy and in active labor, my God!

With my mind and heart racing, I had many questions that plagued my thoughts: What will he look like? Will he have hair? Will I be a good mother? That last question was the most repetitive one that I had. It seemed as if Keta was feeling me overreact. She began to say, "It's going to be alright. Just stay calm."

Keta is the eldest of my mother's six children–one who I would call the backbone of my family. For some reason, the moments that a little girl would have with her mother, I shared them with my sister, Keta. My first school dance, my fifth-grade graduation, her combing my hair–putting colorful burettes on my ponytails. Hmph, memory lane. I feel sad when I think about my childhood memories because

Keta had to bear all of the weight in ensuring that I had support, and all of those major highlights of my life, I lived through with Keta. My mom was in the same household, but it seemed as if my sister was my mom.

Keta was strong, she was stern, and she did not play! When she told me and my other siblings to do something, we knew to get it done. Keta is my confidant. Till this day, I can talk to her without her passing judgment, she listens, and gives sound advice. Even when I don't take her advice, she never holds it against me. Keta was my mother's most responsible kid at an early age. She was a decisive and independent young lady. At the age of 14, she moved out of our mother's house and into her boyfriend's house to help take care of his ill grandmother and his younger siblings. After she left, I felt like me and the rest of my siblings were fucked! Today, Keta is married to that same man, and she is STILL an important pillar in my life.

But here it is, February 1, 2004–Super Bowl Sunday (Panthers VS Patriots) and I'm about to experience the delivery of my first-born child at the age of 20. You mean to tell me that without any guidance or direction in life, I'm about to be responsible for another human being? My thoughts went rampant, but that came to an end once my family arrived, and the hospital staff began prepping me.

My family has been overly excited since coming to know of my pregnancy because most of them never expected to see me carrying a child, let alone give birth to one. That's more than I can say about my son's sperm donor, excuse me, his father—and I use that term loosely.

Since finding out we were pregnant, my son's father, P has been a ghost 90% of the time. P is classified as a deadbeat. You know, the one who lacks morals and responsibility and who shows up to shake me down for half of the lawsuit for a child he ain't done NOTHING for! And that is why I haven't bothered to inform him that I am in labor. Furthermore, he's going to make me angry and cause my blood pressure to rise. But I guess I'll call and let him know tomorrow.

The door swings open and Dr. Sullivan walks through asking, "Ms. Shelby, are you ready?"

"As ready as I can be," I replied with a smile. After laboring to push my son into this cruel world, he made his entrance at 9:45 AM. I stared into the big brown prettiest eyes, with eyelashes full as if he was a girl. Look at this high yellowed, little boy—weighing nine pounds and eight ounces, with a head full of curly black hair. What will I name him?

I knew I would name him Nigel. Nigel is an English originated name that means champion. Beyond that, it is a more valuable name to me because it was the name of one of my childhood best friends. My friend lost his life in a terrible car accident as a teenager so it's only right that I honor him. But of course, he needs a middle name. Ahmad…Yeah, Ahmad sounds good with that. Y'all, I watched the movie "Soul Food" nearly every day, and one of the characters' names is Ahmad. That name is an Arabic name that means most praised. Most Praised Champion, yeah, I like that. Nigel Ahmad Shelby.

With a perfect name and a perfect little face, I couldn't stop staring at him. He's so beautiful. I can't believe that I made something so precious. God must favor me to bless me with something so perfect. My motherly instincts kicked in instantly. Loving Nigel and caring for him came so naturally to me. I didn't want the nurses to take him to the nursery, but mama needed some rest, I guess. So, I finally agreed to let the nurse take him.

After waking up from my nap, I decided that I'd address the elephant that has yet to enter the room. I began to dial his phone number. Ring. Ring. Ring.

"Hello," he says. The sound of his voice automatically irritated my soul, and I spoke with an attitude and snappy tone the entire conversation.

Me: "Umm, P, is your mom home?"

P: "No, she's at work. What's up?"

Me: "Well, tell her I had the baby."

P: "You did? When? Where are you? Why are you just now calling," he asked with concern in his voice.

Me: "Ummm, we are at the Women and Children Center. And I had him yesterday." As soon as I said my last word, I ended the call abruptly.

A few hours passed by then P walked in with his daughter Tee. Nigel's only sister at the time. She was so excited to see her little brother. Her face lit up with a smile as she asked, "Can I hold him?" Tee's interaction with Nigel was enough for me to let go of all the anger that I was feeling towards their dad. At least in that moment. Should have known that moment would be temporary.

Not even a few days later, I started to hear the rumors that were surfacing about P true thoughts of Nigel. One rumor stated that P said that Nigel was too yellow to be his son. He even said Nigel's dad was white. Laughing my ass off, the nerve of this clown! How could you deny something so precious that God blessed you with? Your first-born son at that.

JUST A SPERM DONOR

One day, while chilling outside with my cousin Nikki and her friend Chris, he decided that he wanted to play matchmaker. In mid conversation, Chris says, "I got this homeboy that I want you to meet, Mika."

You know, back then we did the whole I'm gon' hook my homegirl up with your homeboy type shit. Sometimes it worked out; sometimes it didn't. In this particular case, I agreed to meet the homeboy. When I first saw him, I thought, ok, he's cute. He was brown skinned and slim. There was something special about his eyes that were very attractive to me. To be honest, his eyes said a hell of a lot. They were giving, come get me, and Mika, you better run–at the same time.

Had I known then what I know now, y'all, I would've looked at them eyes and ran the other way. How can the devil smile at you and look like an angel? Like Taylor Swift said, 'I should've known he was trouble when he walked in."

P and I talked on the phone and kicked it from time to time. The vibe that we shared went well together. The only factor that stood in between us was that neither of us had a place that we lived at alone. I'd never been out on my own, but I lived with my grandmother after graduating from "Job Corps." I honestly didn't like living there, but that's what it was. Don't get me wrong, my grandmother and I were close, but it was something about the feeling of being grown but laying under someone else's roof that didn't click with me. I needed my own shit, and I needed it ASAP.

I worked two jobs, so I had the income to pay for a place to live, but that wasn't enough. I needed some credit history. Without hesitation, P asked his mom to co-sign our first apartment, and she agreed. We got settled in our new home and still managed to vibe the same way we had been vibin'. Three months passed, and we still hadn't had sex yet. I felt like he was such a gentleman to not pressure me for sex. I would soon find out that there was no pressure because he was sleeping with someone else the entire time.

My relationship started off so good with P. One night P and I traveled to Kroger's off Oakwood, in Huntsville, Alabama to pick up ingredients for a taco salad. As we were walking down an aisle looking for chips, we started a conversation about our relationship. We were focused on our future—moving in together and starting a family.

P suddenly says, "I want to have a son."

He already had a 2-year-old daughter at the time, so I guess a son would have sealed the deal for him. Of course, I was with it, so we decided to submit a prayer request to God while in Kroger.

We both said to God, "Please allow us to have a baby." I continued to pray, "Lord, please give me an opportunity to carry a baby full term and bring the baby into the world." Now, how did we go from a conversation to a small prayer in this old and dirty looking Kroger.

One of my biggest fears and one of my deepest sadness was not being able to carry a child full term. I lost babies—that shit was hurtful. The thought of me not being able to bear a child was too much for me. I worked at a production plant called Cinram where we packaged CD's and DVD's. It was a pretty easy job as far as the workload, but they worked our ass on 12-hour shifts and the pay was bullshit. Like any other warehouse job, it was messy, and everyone was fucking everyone.

I happened to get sick while at work one day, so I called P to pick me up to take me to the hospital. This nigga actually picked me up and dropped me off at the hospital. That should've been my first red flag for him. If your girl is sick, why wouldn't you stay at the hospital with her?

After sitting in the back awaiting the doctor to come in, he walked in and said,

ER Doctor: "You're not feeling so well are you?"

Me: "No, I have been dizzy, feeling sick to my stomach…"

ER Doctor: Interrupting my speaking,"Yeah, your breasts are sore."

Me: "Yeah, How do you know?"

ER Doctor: "Yeah, you're pregnant."

Me: "Huh?"

Hearing those words had to be the craziest thing. It was scary but also exciting.

I prayed, "God, please just let me carry this baby full term."

There were days that I laid in my bed crying because my baby daddy was stressing me out. So, my prayers continued and changed to, "Lord, don't let this stress affect my child." My relationship with P was a short lived one. After four months of my pregnancy, I was done with him mentally, physically, and emotionally. I couldn't stand the thought of P. It'd gotten so bad from the cheating, to lying, to flat out disrespect, and when I thought things couldn't get any worse, they did.

One day me and Nikki were at home, at my apartment, and I decided to prepare lunch for me, her, and P. I cooked chicken wings and fries that day. While P was in the shower, his phone was ringing off the hook, so I decided to see who was calling. It could've been an emergency or something. Wrong! It was a bitch calling and texting him. When he got out of the shower, while handing him his plate, I asked, "Who is this bitch texting your phone?" From there, an argument started.

In the midst of us arguing I sat down on the couch. And suddenly, a ranch bottle came flying across the room and landed on my stomach. I had a clear Nokia phone with a clear Tweety Bird case– so when my phone rang, you could see it light up. It seemed as if as soon as the ranch bottle connected with my stomach, my phone lit up and vibrated.

I threw my phone at P, but before the phone could hit him, I'd already football-tackled his ass. Nikki instantly jumped into the fight. We beat his ass! The funny thing is–after we beat his ass, that n*gga still had that plate of chicken in his hands. He NEVER dropped it; his greedy ass! But from that day forward, I never had to worry about him putting his hands on me again.

After the fight, P left our apartment in such a hurry–still with his plate in his hands. I watched him as he ran down the stairs and hopped into his Fuchsia Pink 1999 Crown Vic with Silver 22-inch rims. While staring out the window, reality started to set in about what just transpired. So, I instantly got worried about him hitting me in my stomach and wanted to go get checked out of course. After going to the emergency room, I learned that Nigel was just fine so I went home to get some rest for work the next day.

After working a 10-hour shift, I came home to an empty ass apartment. P took every-fucking-thing out of our apartment. I guess since his mom paid for the bullshit, he felt that he could take it. He literally took it all! I mean groceries and ALL! Can y'all believe this nigga? At that moment, I knew that he didn't mean me any good. We have never been together since, and neither have I bothered him as a father.

P stupid ass took being Nigel's father for granted Nigel's entire life. I feel as if I even took my role as Nigel's mother for granted at times too, however the difference is, I never left Nigel's side and I never stop being his mom–that's way more than P can ever say.

A JOURNEY DOWN MEMORY LANE

I spent most of the first days as a mother admiring Nigel. It's like you never fully know how to be a mother because everyday life is different. Besides that, Nigel started daycare at six weeks old 'cause mama had to go back to work, and we don't know where daddy is at. I was finally getting used to feeding and changing diapers. Before I knew it, the babbling came—ma-ma. Yaaay! He's calling my name. After crawling, the walking came. And in no time, he was running around full speed. He was growing before my eyes.

Nigel's first words were, "One point five." And if you're wondering what one point five is, it's the amount of grams that a bag of weed used to cost for $10. Now, I know you're probably wondering, why in the fuck was his first words one point five. Well, it's because Nigel's mom sold weed during this time. So, Nigel was hearing the term one point five a lot. It got so bad to the point where those words became one of his nicknames. He had many. Nigel used to get up every morning and say, "One point five," then waited on someone to say it back. That's how he knew that someone else was awake. The project's apartments that we lived in were so small, and the rooms were in close vicinity with thin walls. You could hear anything someone said. So, Nigel would stand in his crib hollering, "One point five," wait for someone to say it back, then he'll get out of his crib and come in the room smiling.

One day he went to daycare saying the same thing. Oh my Gosh. Why Nigel?

When I picked him up, the teacher asked, "What is he saying?" I said, "Ma'am, I don't know." But thinking to myself, Lady, my baby is trying to tell you how to weigh a sack. It was important to me to give Nigel all the things I didn't have access to as a child. My mom had 6 kids and I only had one, so I felt I had no excuses. I saw a lot of things that I shouldn't have as a child–when trying to find my way, and I needed to make life different for him.

One of Nigel's gifts for his second birthday was a PlayStation Portable Player (PSP). They'd just hit the scene, so all of the kids wanted one. My mom said, "Why would you do that? He's not even old enough to know what it is." That's how you know he was too young. However, he figured it out. The PSP came with a disk that I didn't attempt to look at. I basically just put it in and allowed Nigel to figure it out. Until one day the daycare teacher called me and said, "You need to come up here because we need to talk."

With sighs, I asked, "What has he done now?"

I always felt that Nigel would be bullied due to him being smaller than the average kid in his age group percentile. I was so scared for him so that's where my mind automatically went. The teacher proceeded to say, "I just need you to come up here to talk about Man-Man."

"Okay," I responded.

Man-Man was also one of the nicknames that Nigel had.

I stopped what I was doing and went to the daycare to speak with his teacher. After arriving and sitting down to speak with her, she said, "I told everybody to take a nap and Nigel said that he didn't want to. I walked out of the classroom and came back, and Nigel had pulled his pull-up down and shitted on the floor."

Disturbed as fuck, I said, "What? This is so out of the ordinary for Nigel 'cause Nigel doesn't even wanna get his shoes dirty! So what do you mean Nigel shitted on the floor?"

She said, "He pulled his pull-up off and shitted on the floor, girl."

Oh my gosh, I am so embarrassed. I just looked at her and looked at Nigel's big headed ass and he dropped his head.

I then said, "Nooney, you know you're in trouble, right?"

"Ok, mommy."

We left the daycare center and got in the car. I asked Nigel, "Why did you do that?"

"That's what Stuey did when he got mad."

Y'all, hold on! I didn't know who the hell Stuey was so I called my mama.

Me: "Ma! Guess what Nigel did at school."

My Mom: "What, girl?"

I told her and she said,

My Mom: "Mika, You been letting him watch Family Guy?"

Me:"Family Guy? The little show that came on the little disk for his PSP Player?"

Ok, now why would y'all include Family Guy in a game that's created for children? I hadn't ever seen Family Guy, but the disk had the entire season one on his game. My child is watching this shit repeatedly because it's inside of his PSP Player.

My mama said, "Mika, you're so retarded. Watch Family Guy and call me back." And just so happen, the episode that I watched, the dog was fantasizing about fucking the mama. Listen, when I saw that shit, I was like, oh my goooosh! So, that's who Stuey is. Y'all, I literally thought Stuey was a kid at daycare that Nigel saw shitting on the floor and decided to mock.

As parents, please control what your child is watching and pay attention to the parental advisory label as well. I literally thought that because this little disk with a dog on the front came with that PSP player for kids. Regardless, if that game had an age restriction on there or not—and I highly doubt that it did, there shouldn't have been an adult TV show included on something that children had access to. It was advertised for kids. Some grown creative people are sick as fuck in the mind, and we need to watch what people are doing to our kids. However, I was a young new mom who didn't know what Family Guy was. All I knew was, I wanted my child to have the game that all of the kids wanted. I didn't give a damn if he wasn't old enough to have it. Sadly, that was my mindset.

The first two years of Nigel's life, I had the struggles of an average black, single mother. After being evicted from the apartment that I shared with P, I had to move to Northwood projects. But right before Nigel turned three, I started thriving. I was introduced to a colleague who taught me a new trade that was popping. Me and Nigel went from struggling to not wanting for shit. I worked hard—15 to 16 hours daily. I had to keep up with the lifestyle that we were becoming accustomed to.

FEBRUARY 1, 2007

Ecstatic to start Nigel's birthday off I went into his room to wake him up, "Good morning, Nooney!"

Before he could open his eyes, he began smiling and said, "Good morning, Mommy!" He stared at me in total admiration with those big bright eyes of his. Pulling down his shirt to his matching Spider-Man pajamas, he crawled over to sit in my lap. As Nigel gave me the biggest hug, I asked, "Do you know what today is?"

He giggled,

Nigel: "Yes, it's my birthday."

Me: "Yes, it is! Happy Birthday baby! We are going to have so much fun today. First, we're going to eat, then we're going to go party."

Nigel: "Ok, Mommy!" Nigel jumped from my lap and started running towards his bedroom door. I walked behind him. Before entering the kitchen, I stopped and turned on the TV. SpongeBob, of course. While Nigel sat on the couch with his legs folded Indian style, I prepared breakfast. As usual, I dressed Nigel first then dressed myself so that we could go celebrate. Nigel was extremely happy and so energetic running around because we were celebrating his birthday at Chuck E. Cheese. He must've called my name a thousand times.

"Mama, Mama, Mama," is what he said repeatedly. His pretty smile and squeakiest little voice were so cute.

Chuck E. Cheese was a thing for children, so he celebrated his first four birthdays there. For Nigel's fifth birthday, he wanted to go skating, so we did that. While skating, he kept falling, laughing and getting back up. He has always been the silliest kid.

When Nigel was about 4 or 5, he loved SpongeBob so I took him to a Burger Parlor called "Cheeseburger Cheeseburger." They sold burgers, fries, and the shakes that came inside of the tall glass. The restaurant reminded you of the 50s type vibes because staff wore the poodle skirts, button down shirts, and ribbons in their hair. After being seated, our waitress came to the table and asked what we wanted to order. I told her my order then she looked over at Nigel and enthusiastically said, "Aww, he's so cute. What are you going to have, little man?"

With so much excitement, Nigel looked up at her with his big bright eyes and asked the waitress, "Do y'all have Krabby Patties?"

She seemed so confused while asking, "Huh?"

"Do y'all sell Krabby Patties," Nigel asked again?

Still confused as hell, she looked up at me and said, "Krabby Patties. What is he talking about?"

Me: "Girl, you ain't ever seen SpongeBob?"

Waitress: "Nooo."

Me: "Oh well, you're not going to know what he's talking about." During the Fall of 2009, Nigel started kindergarten, and I was so nervous because he was so little. I just knew he was the smallest person in his classroom. I remember his first day of kindergarten like it was yesterday. I still have pictures from that day too.

He wore some denim shorts, a plaid button down shirt, and some all white K-Swiss. I used to love the little kids all white K-Swiss 'cause they were so cute. Nigel had his little book bag with the character Diego on it. We proceeded to walk into the school and Nigel was so excited with his little head moving from side to side.

We arrived at the door as the staff greeted us and asked his name. Nigel then said, "Bye mommy," in the most exciting voice.

Although I was nervous, I smiled and said, "Have a great day baby." When it was time for me to pick him back up, he talked the entire ride home. He loved to talk. The higher his voice got, the squeakier it became as he talked. It was just the cutest little thing to hear him talk about his day. And as time went on, I thought that Nigel would be a follower. I was wrong.

In his younger days, Nigel was what I would call a ring leader. When he would come home from school, I'd ask, "Did you have a happy face or a sad face today, Nigel?"

He'd respond enthusiastically, "A happy face!" Whenever I pulled his folder out, I'd see a sad face on his behavior chart.

"Nigel, what did you do?"

"The teacher said I won't stop talking."

I knew my child so of course; I knew what his problem was. Nigel never stopped talking. His teachers would tell me that he was a good child, but he just won't stop talking. I had to face the fact, no one was shutting Nigel up. But throughout the years, Nigel grew a great love for school.

Aside from talking, he performed exceptionally well in school academically. He decided to join the band when he entered fifth grade and stuck with it as he moved to each grade. The first instrument that he played was the clarinet, and he also played the flute as well. Nigel tested really well on drums, but he wasn't feeling it because it was "too heavy." He gave basketball a try, but I could tell he wasn't really into it. The children would be on the court and Nigel would be far away on the sidelines. When his teammates attempted to throw him the ball, he'd be zoned out. He was present but not there so I didn't force him to be a sports kid. That wasn't Nigel.

Instead, Nigel wanted to be on the cheerleading squad so I allowed him to be. He tumbled after they cheered, and he loved it. There were so many layers to Nigel.

Nigel went through a phase where he loved a few movies and TV Shows. He loved Shrek and SpongeBob. And oh my gosh, we must've watched Spider-Man a thousand times. Nigel also wanted to dress me and do my hair. He even had a phase of all things with Beyoncé. I guess that obsession came from me because I listened to Beyoncé's music throughout my entire pregnancy. Her album with the song "Me, Myself, & I" on it was my therapy. I worked my entire pregnancy; so yeah, I needed Beyoncé's music as an escape from reality.

Nigel always wanted me to wear my hair like Beyoncé and dress like Beyoncé. He was just Beyoncé crazy. And boy oh boy! Beyoncé and Nicki Minaj became friends. Nicki is my all time favorite so y'all know how me and Nigel were getting down together in the car listening to classics like, "Feeling Myself" and "Flawless." He was literally my little best friend, and I wanted to give him what I never had plus more.

Nigel got a chance to experience everything that I didn't experience as a child. He has also gone to places that some children can only imagine going like Six Flags, DisneyLand, many beaches, Walt Disney World, and many other places. Those things alone are a blessing because as his mom, I hadn't been to many places outside of Alabama as a child.

While I've mentioned surface leveled attributes of Nigel, I must mention the fact that Nigel was so kind hearted. I can recall at either the age five or six, Nigel showed me that he was a giver at heart. One day while we were heading inside of the dollar store, a homeless man was sitting outside.

Compassionately, Nigel asked, "Mama, Can we buy him something out the store?"

"Yes, baby. We can." I won't ever forget that we bought the man some Pringle's and a soda. But when we came back outside, the homeless man was gone. Nigel was so upset that he cried.

"Mama, can we please find him," Nigel asked?

His little spirit melted my heart, and the fact that he was upset, I couldn't go home without finding the man. So, we rode around until we found him. When we found the man, I rolled the window down, and so excited with a smile on his face, Nigel yelled, "I got something for you!" It was so cute. Nigel handed the man his Pringle's and drink, and the man thanked him. Nigel turned around and looked at me with the brightest smile. I knew at that moment that my son was special. He felt so fulfilled after doing his good deed. I knew that Nigel had my heart.

There aren't many kids who think that way. Like, seriously, Nigel was in tune with his emotion at such a young age, and it did my spirit well. He remained the same as he continued to live.

Nigel was always a joker, but as he got older, he used to get on my nerves. For instance, he always called me bruh and that shit used to make me so mad. I used to say, "Nigel, if you call me bruh one more time, ima knock your ass out."

He would just laugh. It didn't matter how loud I yelled or how angry I was, he would just laugh and say, "Ma, why you doing all that?" Nigel loved me so much.

Growing up, he'd say things like: "I'm going to take care of you, mama. Mama, do you need anything? Are you okay, mama?" Nigel spent a lot of time just making sure that I was happy and that I knew how much he loved me. Just as well as I knew he loved me, I made sure that he knew how much I loved him. But one thing that

always made me sad was the fact that I couldn't give him what P
should have.

SOMEONE TO CALL DAD

P's mother moved within the first two years of Nigel's life. So, he never got a chance to know his grandmother or any of his dad's family. However, Nigel did have a man in his life who took care of him, and he also did the things with Nigel that a biological dad should've done.

On the first day that I met Que, there was an instant attraction. I met him inside a club through a home girl of mine named Kaye. Me and Kaye stayed on the club scene. And one night while at the Bench Warmer's Club, I asked her who had weed. She said Que but I didn't know who Que was so she pointed him out and we both walked up to him.

Kaye asked Que, "You good?"

"Yeah," he replied.

"Well, this is my homegirl Mika and she wants some."

Que went inside his pocket and pulled out a sack of weed then put it in my hand.

"How much do I owe you," I asked?

"Nothing," he replied.

I froze for a moment but it wasn't because of the free weed, it was when we locked eyes. This man was so sexy to me. Dark skinned, slim, low haircut, with a mouth full of gold. Que knew how to dress, and he always wore colors so well. He was well put together, and he had hustler written all over him. When he said nothing, his girlfriend overheard him. She instantly started to act crazy—yelling at him and all types of shit. To the average woman, that would have been a red flag. But to me, it was intriguing. I wanted to know who he was. For his girlfriend to be acting the way that she was acting over a simple sell, my mind automatically thought, He must be working with something down there? Let's see what's happening here.

Please don't judge me; I was about 22 or 23 at the time young. My thought process now would've told me to run. That one night turned into years of drama. There were times where Que had issues with my ex, and there were times that I had issues with his ex. Guns were pulled. Fights happened. His ex even tried to run me off the road with her car one night. Honey, I can't make this shit up. But, the more drama we went through, the closer me and Que became.

The relationship between me and Que has always been loving and very open. There will always be a connection there. After me and him went our separate ways, he still continued to be a father to my son. Que was attentive with my son—he talked to my baby, and got to know and understand my baby. We both knew that Nigel would probably be gay when he got older because of how he carried himself. Que never made my baby feel no type of way about it. He loved his "Magician" no matter what. *Laugh out loud* That's the nickname that he gave Nigel because Nigel went through a phase where everything was about magic tricks.

Nigel loved Que and his family, and they all loved Nigel back.

Sometimes I wonder what our life would be like if we never parted ways. I can remember pure happiness when Que and I were together. Sometimes I still envision Que walking Nigel to school when we lived across the street from Nigel's elementary school. It would do my heart well seeing the two of them bond. Things that Nigel never did with his biological dad.

Nigel had a need for Que, and Que fulfilled that need for Nigel.

It takes a special man to raise another man's child. And an even more special one to part ways with that same child's mother, and still make an effort to be in that child's life. I will always love and respect Que for that. I thank God that my baby had him as a father figure for those six years of Que being a free man.

After Que went to prison, I moved on with my relationship life. But when he was released, he still came and picked Nigel up to hang with him, took him to the barbershop, and did other things that fathers did. In 2012, me and Nigel moved to Muscle Shoals, and we lost contact with Que. By the time Nigel and I moved back to Huntsville, Que had gotten into some trouble and was heading back to prison. Nigel didn't get to see him before he left.

Que is currently incarcerated, and he was incarcerated at the time of Nigel's death so he couldn't attend his funeral. When Que saw Nigel's death on the news, he found a way to contact me. Que took Nigel's death really hard. When I speak with Que till this day, it's still hard for him to process Nigel not being here. For one, he didn't get a chance to say goodbye. And two, Que still has trouble processing that his first son is no longer on earth. Que has had two children since we've dated. Yes, he has his own biological son, but that didn't change the love he shared with Nigel. He still says that Nigel will always be his first son and I'm thankful for that.

THE KNOWING

As Nigel started to come into his own identity, I sat back and noticed that he wasn't like your average little boy. He wasn't into cars, sports, or action figures. He was into sentimental or soft things per say. I remember seeing a picture that my sister had taken of him at her house holding a magazine with a picture of Beyoncé on it. His little face lit up because he loved Beyoncé. As his mother, I knew that he was gonna be gay. The hardest part was having to defend him at such a young age. Nigel was only 4 years old.

Nigel didn't want to do things that little boys wanted to do. He was more interested in the things that girls wanted to do. And to feel that I had to come to his defense about his preferences was hard and heavy on me. It even caused me to have issues in past relationships. My boyfriend at the time would say that the way I disciplined Nigel was "too soft." The fact that I used to show Nigel affection or baby him up as some would say, was also a problem. People would make comments like: "He's a boy; let him cry. Boys cry; you don't have to baby him up. You gon' make that child gay."

The only thing that went through my mind was, How in the hell do you make a child gay?

I didn't care anything about Nigel being a boy. If my child was hurting, he needed to be comforted. My nurturing made him feel loved, and that's what everyone should want as a parent. Seeing my baby hurting hurts me. Regardless of his gender, that's how I saw it. But because I knew he was softer than what society would want him to be, I catered to his needs. The world wouldn't ever do that. That alone became a problem to many of my affiliates.

Say for instance, a parent has a son and the son picks up a Baby Doll. The parent's first response is scolding, "No, boys don't play with dolls!" That's a child, and that child is not sitting there thinking that playing with a doll will make him gay. That's literally a kid! Their brains don't work like that. It becomes a problem because adults make it a problem. A little boy's brain does not tell him, "I wanna stick my dick inside of another man because I'm playing with this doll."

That's adult bull shit. We as adults project bull shit on our kids. Adults are the problem, not the kids. Childrens' thoughts are pure and innocent. As a parent, it is your duty to speak to your children respectfully.

Me and Nigel had an open and transparent relationship. I never sugarcoated anything with him. At the age of 10, I'd always ask him, "Ahmad, are you gay?"

His response would be, "No, mom. Why are you asking me that? Stop asking me that." After those responses, I stopped asking him because I could tell that I was making him uncomfortable. When I stopped asking, it allowed him the space to be comfortable and come to me when he was ready.

Sometimes I would sit in my car awhile before going inside after arriving home from work. This particular day, Nigel must've looked out of the window and saw that I was outside. He called my phone.

Nigel: "Hey mom."

Me: "Hey baby!"

Nigel: "How was work?"

Me: "It was good!"

Nigel: "Mom, I wanna talk to you about something."

Me: "Ok, I'm finna come inside."

Nigel: "No, I actually wanna come out and sit in the car."

Me: "Ok." So, he came outside, opened the door, and sat inside of my green Chrysler Sebring. Nigel smiled at me and proceeded to talk to me.

Nigel: "I love you."

Me: "I love you too."

Nigel: "I got something I need to talk to you about."

Me: "Ok, what is it?"

Nigel: "Mom. I'm attracted to boys and girls."

Me: "Ok Nigel. What you wanna eat?"

Nigel: "Rick's Barbecue."

Me: "Ok. Put your seatbelt on."

Nigel grabbed me and hugged me so tight. We pulled off and drove to Rick's Barbecue for dinner, and our conversation didn't continue about Nigel's confirmation to his sexuality. I don't know what he was expecting me to say, but I always knew. I was waiting for him to tell me for himself after asking so many times and him denying it. I guess I had to stop asking in order for him to build up enough courage to tell me the truth. Nigel was 13 when he came to talk to me about his sexuality. One thing that I would never do is act as if I didn't know my child. I watched his movement and the way that he carried himself. It was always a lot more feminine than your average boy. With that being said, again, I was waiting on him to tell me.

I remember a little girl that Nigel had a crush on. For Valentine's Day he would ask me to buy her gifts, and I did. So, whatever Nigel was feeling was ok with me. I'm going to be supportive because he's my son. When Nigel was 14, there was a boy who lived in the same neighborhood as we did—who called himself crushing on Nigel. One day he came and knocked on our door with boldness.

"Is Nigel home?"

I responded and yelled, "Hold on. Nigel come here!"

Nigel came running down the stairs. When the little boy saw Nigel, he smiled and handed Nigel a Taco Bell bag.

The little boy said, "Here. I got this for you!"

Nigel rudely said, "I don't eat Taco Bell!"

I said, "Ahmad, apologize because you don't do nothing like that."Nigel was so tickled while saying, "But mom I don't eat it."

"That's not the point. It's the fact that he went out of his way to think about you."

The little boy finally said, "It's okay if he doesn't eat it."

I said, "I'll eat it just because you got it. Thank you." Nigel closed the door on the little boy. I looked at Nigel and said, "Nigel, don't do him like that. Even if you don't like him, he still thought about you."

"Imma eat it mama, but I already know my stomach gonna be hurting."

A short time later, the same little boy came knocking on my door with some Takis Chips. Nigel was definitely with that because he loved Takis. After he received the chips, he said to me, "That was more like it," with that big pretty smile on his face. Nigel shared his first experience of kissing a little boy with a friend of mine and not me. My friend at the time stated that Nigel was so dramatic while telling the story. He was a dramatic person anyway. I laughed hysterically because Nigel said that the boy's lips were dry. It's so funny to me because Nigel always carried lip balm. He wasn't going anywhere without it. I honestly believe that he got that from me.

The only difference between the two of us was that I like the tubes, and Nigel liked the one that you have to stick your finger in. I hate that kind because the balm gets underneath your nails.

Nigel loved weird shit. He was nerdy, preppy, and a little hood. If we went to Toys R' US, and I said, "Ok Nigel, you can get anything out of here electronic wise."

Nigel would come back with slime or anything that the average child wouldn't want. Of all of the things that you could've chosen, you decided to choose slime? Ok Nigel.

When it was time for me to buy Nigel games for his PlayStation, he never chose a common game like MineCraft or FortNite. He'd always come back with something I never seen or heard of.

"Nigel, what is that?

"I don't know, but it looks cool."

Some people tend to think that just because children are weird that they are pushovers, TUH! That wasn't Nigel's case.

One time my sister Lily called me and said, "Oh my gosh, Mika! Nigel just came in here with blood all over his shirt. Some little boy was picking on Travez so Nigel beat him up and busted his nose. Now I'm probably about to have to whoop the little boy's mama."

Nigel would defend himself if he had to, but he would rather not. It would have to get to the point where someone had to hit him first. Nigel wouldn't ever swing first. I was always the total opposite because I'd pass the first punch. I never gave anyone the chance to get one up on me. In contrast, Nigel was a lover; he never wanted conflict. He always said I reacted too hastily and was the reason he chose not to tell me certain things.

SILENT CRIES

While Nigel was sweet, he also had a dark side as he became a teenager. Oftentimes, I would become frustrated. I just didn't understand it. He went through this phase to where he didn't want to come outside. From 2018 through 2019, it was an emotional roller coaster. Nigel started fighting in school, but he never told me that he didn't want to go to school because they were bullying him. He basically made it seem as if he didn't want to go to Huntsville High because we'd just moved back to Huntsville, and he was missing the life that he had in Florence, Alabama.

I always allowed Nigel to vacation in Florence each Summer since he was a baby. So, I expected him to go once school was out. Summer was ending and my sister Lily called me on the phone asking crazy ass questions. As I answered the phone, Nigel said, "Mama, don't get mad. I just wanna ask you something."

I asked, "What?"

Nigel asked, "Can I stay here with auntie Lily and go to school?"

"I don't know, Nigel."

Nigel has never been away from me during the school year, so I didn't know how to feel about that question being asked. But I remember Lily saying, "Please, just let him stay with me." I finally agreed to it. I didn't know that I would eventually regret it. The reason that I regret my decision is because Nigel was in a fragile state of mind, and I allowed him to tell me that staying in Florence was best for him. It wasn't.

Nigel's anxiety levels increased. I recall my sister calling me saying, "I don't know what's wrong with Nigel, but he keeps saying that he smells bad. I keep telling him no he doesn't, but he won't believe it." Come to find out, someone at school said something of that nature to him, and it stuck with him. He wouldn't let go of this kid telling him he stinks, and my baby's anxiety made him obsessed with thinking he did. He was having anxiety to the point that I was scared. I didn't know anything about anxiety then. Nigel stopped going to school while he was living with my sister. One day she called and said, "Nigel didn't go to school again."

At that very moment, I knew that it was time for Nigel to move back home. And because God works in mysterious ways, Lily's house caught fire. I had to pick up Nigel sooner than I intended to get him. He lived with my sister for about four months that year, and I never imagined that it would be his last visit. When Nigel came back home, he was just different. He didn't want to come out of his room. He didn't want to go outside. He kept telling himself that he stinks. He would say, "Mama, smell me."

I always smelled him and reassured him that he didn't have an odor. Those thoughts had taken over him to the point of me being so scared. I had to break down and finally get him treated. It became routine for Nigel to see a therapist, because the Psychiatrist that I took him to see diagnosed him with Severe Obsessive-Compulsive

Disorder (OCD). She explained that he was obsessing, thinking that he smelled bad. He took so many showers daily, and he changed clothes so much that it would piss me off. Simply because I had so many clothes to wash.

I didn't know how to handle Nigel's behaviors. I tried my best not to get frustrated, but I couldn't help it 'cause I didn't understand it. I didn't understand the anxiety, how deep issues were within Nigel, or what he was going through in totality. In the process of me trying to be understanding, I also need him to do what he's supposed to do as a child. He didn't do it. One day while I was at work, a member from the administration team called me and said Nigel wasn't at school. I had to leave work to see if Nigel was at home and safe.

First, let me just say this. He had been asking me if he could watch "Set It Off," and I kept telling him no. I knew how emotional Nigel was, and he wasn't ready to handle the intensity of the movie. Hell, I cry when I watch it.

Y'all, as I walked through the front door, what did I see? Nigel sitting on the couch with his feet kicked up, eating snacks while watching "Set It Off."

Sternly, I said, "Go your ass upstairs and get your toothbrush."

He questioned, "Huh?"

"Go get your toothbrush right now!" He walked upstairs and got his toothbrush then came back downstairs. Afterwards, I instructed him to get in the car. He looked confused; he didn't know what was going on. Next thing you know, we were pulling up at The D-Home (The Detention Center)–a place where troubled kids end up.

"Stay right here, I'll be right back," I said to Nigel. I walked inside and asked the lady sitting at the desk, "Can you get two of your biggest officers to come get my son out of the car 'cause he keeps skipping school. I need y'all to bring him in and take him to the back to scare him like they do on "Scared Straight.""

The lady responded, "Well, because of liability reasons, we can't take him in the back. He has to be in our custody. But I will get them to come outside." Great. I waited for the officers to come out and we walked outside to the car. One officer slung the car door open. Nigel looked surprised as hell.

Both officers yelled sternly, "Get out the car!"

Nigel looked at me and said, "Ma."

"Don't Ma her! Get out the car," the officers yelled! Nigel finally stepped out of the car with an attitude. He was still being himself as we were walking towards the building. As we approached the door, one officer said, "Open the door for your mama."

Nigel said something smart to the officer, so the officer shook him up a little bit. I turned my head as it was happening. If I would've seen Nigel looking sad, I would've broken, and that's not what we went for. The officer yelled one more time, "I said hold the door open for your mama!"

Nigel finally grabbed the door and held it open for me. We entered the building and sat down. The officers were yelling at Nigel continuously and again, I turned my head. They were telling him "If you're not going to school, your mama can go to jail. And she said she ain't going to jail for you. So, if you come in here, you're in our care. We can do whatever to you."

They scared the hell out of my baby. Once we got back in the car, in the sweetest voice, Nigel said, "Mama, can you take me home so I can get dressed and go to school." Nigel got scared to the point where I never had to worry about him skipping school again. I should've been focused on the reason behind Nigel skipping school, but I can admit that it wasn't my focus. That's exactly why I believe that parents should focus on the reasoning behind the actions of children's behaviors instead of the displayed actions. Nigel skipping school wasn't the problem, it was the cause that was really the problem.

While he continued to go to school, I felt that Nigel was changing mentally. It makes me so sad because there were signs, but being uneducated about mental health, I didn't know what to look for. That's why now, if I could leave parents with a message, it would be to get educated about mental health–which includes, signs to look for, best types of treatments, and the learning about your child's specific condition(s). There are different types of triggers, and no two people are the same when it comes to dealing with mental health issues.

One day while having a conversation with me and my best friend, Nigel expressed the fact that he didn't want to live anymore. Nigel was taken back to his psychiatrist and therapist to receive the help that he needed. So, of course, he had to be treated for anxiety and depression. We went to his therapists faithfully after Nigel started to mention suicide. For a long time, I grew worried and removed his room door from the entrance. Yes, I literally removed his door from the hinges so he couldn't be closed in. I also took his cell phone and wouldn't allow him to have any type of contact with the internet because I was scared.

Once his psychiatrist began treating him with Zoloft and Nigel started being Nigel again, I let up on him. I shouldn't have, but I did.

I started asking Nigel questions: "Well, Nigel, what gives you the impression to think that suicide is a way out?"

And he said, "I feel tired and don't belong in this world. People just don't get me."

"Nigel, what do you think that would do to me? Me having to live without you? I may as well die too." Nigel reassured me that he was okay, and everything would be okay.

THE RIGHT TO KNOW

When Nigel was 14, he came to me and said, "Mama, I'm ready to tell my dad." I replied, "Ok, but I'm going to be present for this conversation to make sure that he doesn't react in a way that he shouldn't towards you. But this is still your conversation with your dad."

I proceeded to dial Nigel's sperm donor's phone number.

"Hey, your son wants to talk to you, but he wants to talk face to face. Can you pull up?"

Surprisingly, P pulled up. He knocked, then walked into my house and sat on the couch. Nigel looked at me then looked at his dad.

I calmly said, "Tell him."

Very nonchalantly, Nigel spoke, "Dad, I'm gay."

He was so sarcastic. The Aquarius in him was always shown.

P: "I know that."

Nigel: "Huh?"

P: "I kinda already knew that. I just wanted you to tell me. I don't love you no less—you're my first born son. I still love you the same."

P proceeded to hug Nigel. To be honest, I gained a speck of respect back for his ass because he reacted in a way that made my son feel like he truly loved him. That alone touched me. But of course, his habit of running in and out of Nigel's life diminishes the respect in totality. He would be consistent in coming to see Nigel for a few days and even weeks, then he'd disappear for a year. Finally, he would pop back up and continue the cycle.

Me and Nigel never closed the door on his dad; we always allowed him to come back. I feel like I fucked up in a sense because he wouldn't make a consistent effort with being there for Nigel, but again, we always embraced him. Even when he fucked over us by stealing from us and all of the other shit that he had going, me and Nigel continuously forgave him for everything that he had ever done.

Whenever he popped back up, Nigel's words to me would be, "Mama, just let him stay because you know he's gonna leave again."

And sure enough, his dad would be gone after two or three weeks. P was my only baby daddy, and for five or six years, Nigel was his only son.

I can't seem to wrap my mind around the notion that P never did the right thing by us. Being clear, I released Nigel's dad from my life romantically when I was three months pregnant with Nigel. Leaving me to go through my pregnancy alone, taking all of the furniture from my home while I was at work—all of that shit turned me the fuck off. But because he was my first and only baby daddy, I catered to his needs. For instance, when I worked at the Waffle House, I allowed him to come to my job to get food for him and his bitch simply because he was my baby's dad. I just couldn't turn my back on him. I wasn't fucking him, and I didn't want to fuck him either. That's just what it was.

I've even had plenty of arguments with dudes that I was dating during P's periods of entering and leaving Nigel's life.

The dudes that I was dating wanted to know why I allowed my baby's dad to come in and out whenever he pleased. There would be times where me and my dude would be chilling, and P would call and ask to take a shower.

And of course, my answer would always be yes. One response that I got after allowing him to do so was, "Bitch why? Y'all ain't together. I'm here with you, and you're letting this homeless ass nigga come take a shower?"

My responses to any of them would be full of pity, "That's my son's dad, and he has nowhere else to go." I don't know why, but there's a part of me that always attracts needy types of souls–which is why I thought I could fix Turtle.

When Turtle walked me downstairs to get in the car and go to work, things felt off and I was irritable. Nigel had already been struggling with his anxiety. The night before, we sat and had a conversation about his grades and him attending summer school. Now that I think back, his energy throughout the whole conversation was off. He seemed so disconnected and far away, but he kept assuring me that things would get better. Before heading to work, there was an urgency and need to pray so I said to Turtle, "Bow your head. God put your arms around Nigel, protect him from whatever he's going through, Lord. Just help my baby to not hurt any more. God, please take this darkness from around my child, in Jesus name we pray."

Me: "Amen."

Turtle: "Amen."

Before I continue, let me just tell y'all that Turtle was my best friend. Funny, yeah, I know. Me and Nigel gave Turtle that nickname because he did everything slow—from walking to talking. Turtle was never in a rush to do anything. There was something about our relationship that was more than just your normal friendship.

I met him at a previous job that I had where I was a supervisor in a chicken plant. He had a bachelor's degree, but he was involved with the wrong crowd and went down the wrong path in life. So, I felt like I could save him. There were a lot of things that intrigued me about Turtle.

For starters, the way that he carried himself. And honestly, I didn't view any of these things from a romantic point of view. Embedded in my heart was a sense and feeling of wanting to be there to help Turtle because he would come to work dead drunk. Why in the fuck would he do that? We used knives—knowing damn well you couldn't cut chicken while drunk. I used to cut his chicken for him to keep him from getting fired. So, y'all know that it had to be something special about him for me to be doing DOUBLE THE WORK.

On lunch breaks me and turtle would talk and get to know each other better. He explained that his drinking was a problem because that was what living in a house with all males consisted of. After a few months of being friends, I decided to try and help him, so I discussed with my boyfriend about turtle becoming my roommate. We all worked and hung out together, so my boyfriend knew I had a soft spot for Turtle, and he was okay with him being my roommate.

When he moved in we were really close friends then it became a bond that me, him, and Nigel created. It was because of Nigel that I held on to Turtle for so long. Nigel opened up to him, and he became a comforter to Nigel.

There were times where I just disliked being around Turtle because he wouldn't stop drinking—and that was such a huge turn off to me! When I would be yelling or scolding Turtle for his drinking,

Nigel would notice my actions and say, "Mom, don't do him like that. Don't put him out! You know that he has nowhere to go. He only has us."

So, of course, I went with what Nigel said. The bond that Turtle and I shared had nothing on the bond that he and Nigel shared. And that's what made me continuously try to help with his addiction. But let's continue.

I woke up with extreme irritation so of course, that feeling spilled over into my workday. The job that I was working at the time was with an inventory company. Our daily duties were to travel to different stores to count their inventory. With this job, we were paid according to how much inventory was counted. I was about my money so y'all know I progressed fast. I went from an associate to a driver, and then a supervisor.

I remember getting to work that morning and my supervisor suddenly telling me that I had to drive the sprinter. I was so pissed. The store that I had to drive to for my team's assignment was literally three and a half hours away from where I lived. Mind you, it is four or five o'clock in the morning so it's still dark. To top it all off, some of my employees didn't show up for work so it made us short staffed. Yeah, just add to my irritation.

After waiting to see if more colleagues would show up, we got behind on schedule. So, what do I do? I start speeding to get us there. You're only supposed to go a certain speed in the sprinter. Once you go above the speed limit, the system alerts the company to let them know that you're speeding.

I received a phone call from my supervisor, "Can you slow down? Can you slow down?"

I remember telling my supervisor, "You know after today, I'm stepping down because I'm sick of this shit…Like, I'm irritated as fuck! We're running behind and people are just laying here. You know it is my shift, so I got to be the one to deal with all the shit. It's a lot to handle." Needless to say, we got everything counted and completed the job that day.

On the ride back, I was still irritated, and I still had my mind set on quitting because I'm sick of this shit. I don't get paid enough to deal with the shit that I have to deal with. Not to mention, everybody in this motherfucker on hard-core ass drugs. All types of shit, such as, Soft (cocaine) and pills. Honestly these motherfuckers want whatever it is that you got! Just junkies!

It had gotten so bad to the point that we were going into stores three and four hours away from Alabama and getting put out. Yeah, you read it right. Our overgrown asses were being put out because they were fighting and all types of ghetto and ratchet shit. But as a mother, you know you do what you have to do for your children. Fuck that though! I'll find another job. As those memories plagued my mind while driving, I felt that I should quit, and I continued speeding back to the warehouse. At that point, it was really fuck the job.

As I was driving home, Turtle rings my phone, "Hey, I just got off of work, and I am on my way to the house."

For some reason that is still unknown to this day, my response to Turtle was, "I'm about to pull up in a minute so don't go in the house until I get there."

I pulled up to the house and me and Turtle both got out of our cars and walked in the house. I walked upstairs and called Nigel's name while walking in the bathroom as I do every day. I walked out the bathroom and sat on my bed while noticing that Nigel hadn't come out of his room yet.

Suddenly, I hear Turtle coming up the stairs, so I said, "Turtle, knock on the door and tell Nigel to come here."

I heard Turtle knock on Nigel's door as I asked him. Nigel didn't answer him, so I heard the door open followed by a loud thud and a most gut-wrenching scream, "NOOOOOOOOOOOOOO, EMOJI!" Turtle called Nigel emoji because of his smile.

The pain in his voice echoed through my heart. I immediately knew something wasn't right.

Turtle yelled out, "Mika, call the ambulance."

Before I could call the ambulance, my instincts had gone ahead of me. I ran to Nigel's room. My baby was lying on the floor. His feet were blue. His eyes were open without life in them at all. He was breathing. He had a pulse, but he was unresponsive.

I remember standing there frozen like a statue, hearing Turtle screaming, "Call the ambulance! Call the ambulance!"

As I'm telling this story, I feel myself having an out of body experience. I can see myself running to my bedroom to grab my phone and suddenly dropping to my knees in the hallway. I finally dialed 911.

The replaying of this dispatch's voice is so vivid in my mind right now, calmly she asked, "Can I help you?"

I replied, "My son, send the ambulance. Something is wrong with my son."

At this time, I didn't know what was going on with my son because Turtle removed the belt from his neck so I wouldn't see my son that way when I came into his room. The only thing that I know is he wasn't responsive.

The dispatcher then asks, "Ma'am does he have a pulse?"

I responded hyperventilating, "Ma'am I don't know."

She said, "Ma'am, go see."

I said, "I can't go in there."

"Ok, stay calm."

I proceeded to scream, "Turtle, Turtle, Turtle. Does he have a pulse?"

Turtle yelled, "Yes, he has a pulse and he's breathing, but he's not responsive."

Little did I know that this baby did not have any oxygen to his brain for 30 minutes so that's why he was unresponsive.

I remember yelling at the dispatcher, "Where's the fucking ambulance?" I continued to curse the dispatcher like it was her fault because I didn't know what else to do at the moment. The only thing I knew was to panic. That's it.

Finally, I began hearing the sirens followed by paramedics running up the stairs, telling me, "Move out the way."

After I walked into my bedroom, I called Keta. She answered. I immediately said, "Keta, Keta, something is wrong with Nigel. I don't know what it is, but we're on our way to the hospital."

The next vivid thought that I see is while standing in my bedroom, a police officer steps in and says, "They're going to take him to the hospital, and I need you to stay here." This out of body experience became an inner body experience.

I responded confused as ever, "What?"

"I need you to stay here, ma'am," the officer replied.

With my face discombobulated, "No the fuck I'm not about to stay here. I'm riding in the ambulance with my son!!"

"Ma'am someone has to be here to talk to the investigator."

"Fuck your investigation!!! I'm going to the hospital with my son!"

Turtle stepped into the room and calmly said, "I'll stay here, sir. Please just let her go to the hospital with him."

The officer responded, "OK."

Sirens, sirens, and more sirens. It's like I was in an out of body experience again because all I could see was the ambulance passing me. But the entire time, I'm riding in the front seat. It was raining so hard that I carried the fear of us wrecking before making it to the hospital.

We pulled up to the Women and Children center of Huntsville, Alabama. Of course, they rushed Nigel in and immediately told me to have a seat. I can't recall exactly how long it was. I remember a tall white guy with dark hair walking up to me. I won't ever forget these words because they're an odd choice of words to use in my eyes.

Dr. Selah walked out and said, "Ms. Shelby, I hate to tell you this, but your SON IS GOING TO DIE TONIGHT."

Like what type of shit is that to say. He is only 15. He's a baby. My baby. Lord, Jesus, what is happening? Fading back into reality I hear the doctor's voice, "There is nothing that we can do for him. If you continue to keep him alive, he's going to be a vegetable. He's never going to be a normal kid again because his brain has gone too long without any oxygen."

I instantly took off running. I didn't know where I was going, but I ran out of the hospital into the storm that was taking place outside. I ran into the middle of the parking lot in the pouring rain and just dropped to my knees and screamed! Literally screaming to the top of my lungs. Then I felt someone wrap their arms around me. I looked up, and it was my daddy.

It's something about those words that the doctor said to me that still doesn't sit well with me. At times it makes me wonder, did I ensure that they did all that they could to save Nigel? Those words haunt me every day. He didn't say that my son was already dead. He said that Nigel was GOING TO die. Meaning, at that moment, my baby wasn't dead.

Finally, I started to process why the doctor told me that my son was going to die. In reality, he was saying it is YOUR decision if you're going to keep him alive or let him go. As a mother, how in the fuck do I make this type of decision? I'm going to tell you how. I thought about Nigel.

Nigel was outgoing, silly, always turning flips, rapping, wrestling, and ALWAYS full of life. That's what enabled me to make the decision to let him go. If I hold on to him, he's not going to be Nigel. This was by far the hardest decision I have had to make in life. How do you process leaving the hospital without your child? The SAME place I had given life to a soul was the same place that I had to witness the end of his life.

I remember the lady coming in telling me that they were about to pull the plug on him, and that the funeral home was coming to pick him up so I could go home. I looked up at her and disrespectfully said, "Girl I'm not going nowhere until they come get my child!"

I literally sat there until they arrived to pick him up. Why should I leave? You want to take his organs? Or any type of weird shit. Hell nah, I sat right there until Serenity Funeral Home came and got my baby.

Before the funeral home got there, I can remember after my mom and her husband arrived, and me telling my siblings that I didn't want to see my mom's husband. Lord knows I don't want to disrespect the dead, but I cannot tell Nigel's story without being honest and transparent–without telling the emotions that I felt as a mother, and the emotions that he felt as a child.

I didn't want him to see Nigel because three days before Nigel's suicide, I told Nigel that we were going to Florence to go to church the upcoming Easter weekend.

Me: "Ahmad, we're going to church Sunday with mama nem for Easter.

Nigel: Following a deep sigh of disappointment, "mama please don't make me go down there."

Me: Nigel, don't do that! What is it? Why don't you wanna go to Florence?

Nigel: Mama, I just don't wanna go down there. I don't even wanna go to church.

Me: Whaaaaat? Now, Nigel, why wouldn't you want to go? What is on your mind? Don't start this shit!

Nigel: Ma, I really don't want to tell you this but I don't really want to go to church 'cause I don't want everybody staring at me.

Me: Ahmad, why do you think everybody is gonna be staring at you?

Nigel: 'Cause… Of what G said.

Me: Nigel… I know this is about to piss me off, but what did D say?

Nigel: He basically told me and Kaleigh that we were going to hell for being gay! So, I don't wanna go and everybody starts staring at me.

Me: Nigel, He said what?

Nigel: Mama, you heard me, he was fussing at me, and Kaleigh and he said that we're going to hell for being gay and grandma didn't even say nothin'!

Me: She ain't say nothing to him, Nigel?

Nigel: NOPE! She doesn't ever say anything to him, and G always says stuff to us. And again, she never says NOTHIN'!

Me: Ok, Ahmad, we ain't gotta go down there.

Nigel: Thank you, mama.

During our conversation, I'm literally trying to process why in the hell anyone would say this to a child. Not just anyone. But someone who's supposed to be a Man of God—you shouldn't be judging anybody. And furthermore, no sin is greater than the other; G had a past too. He used to smoke weed, had children out of wedlock, and has been a drinker. I have even smoked blunts with this man before he decided to give his life to Christ so how can you try to condemn my 14-year-old son to hell?

My thoughts remain till this day, if you want me to take you seriously as a Man or Woman of God then you should walk, think, and act as such.

After our conversation, Nigel went upstairs. My baby looked so relieved after he told me those things. Every part of my mind was telling me to call my mama, but I know that my mama gets defensive about her husband, so I didn't call. Had I known that three days later that my child wouldn't be breathing anymore, I would've called.

But yeah, my mom and her husband walked into the room where we all were. As soon as they walked through the door, my Eldest Sister, Marli, on my dad's side, said to my mom, "She don't want him in here." Of course, my mom was feeling all sorts of negative ways mentally because for one, my sister is not her biological daughter.

My sister protected me without knowing my reason. The only fact that she knew was I didn't want G in the room to see my baby. And my mama being the wife that she was, said, "Well, if he's not going to be here then I'm finna go."

Keta looking pissed off yet sternly says, "If your mama walks out this door with this man then I'm done with her—FOR GOOD! And I'm not playing! If she chooses to put this man in front of you and Nigel, I'm done with her." My flesh wanted to say fuck G because the conversation that I had with Nigel started to replay in my mind. There shouldn't have ever been a conversation about Nigel's sexuality without me being present because I'm his mother, and you're not even his blood. You're married into this family. My blood was boiling at this point, and I wanted to say those very words to G, but I held my peace.

I still don't know if mama heard Keta or not but what I do know is. Mama didn't leave. Finally, after gathering my thoughts, I allowed G to go in and see Nigel. No matter how my flesh wanted to leave G out, my heart wouldn't allow me to be that way. Although I don't know the extent of the conversation Nigel, Kaleigh, and G had, my heart will always do what's best for Nigel. But just in case Nigel interpreted the conversation in a way that G didn't mean it, I'm going to give him the benefit of the doubt and allow him to see Nigel. Especially since he's not leaving the hospital with us. Everyone deserves to say their goodbyes; however, I haven't forgotten, and this conversation is going to be had.

I never found the perfect time to have the conversation with G about Nigel. G had fallen ill and had to have open heart surgery then Covid-19 entered into his body. After those events happened, G died so I had to let the conversation die with him. God rest his soul. My niece told me that G had in fact spoken the things that Nigel said he said to them. So, that had to be enough closure for me.

We as black people and as human period have to stop pointing the finger and judging people in totality because we don't agree with what they agree with. I won't ever know what all G said, but I know that it was damaging as fuck to my child.

When you're dealing with kids who are fragile or emotional as Nigel, words affect them deeply and differently. They have pure and kind hearts so anything may hurt them and turn them away.

My son was raised in the church, and for him to say that he didn't want to go back because of someone else's words, is equivalent to failing a child. As adults we need to hold ourselves accountable and be slow to speak–especially when it comes to children because their minds are like sponges. The information that you're giving out as an adult is received in their young minds differently; you can't expect them to interpret a mature conversation with an immature mentality. With that being said, watch your tone, gestures, facial expressions, and how you're relaying the message overall.

After all of that took place, Keta drove me home and the rest of the family followed behind us in their cars. As soon as I walked through my apartment's door, Turtle was sitting on the couch looking defeated—slumped over with his head inside of his hands. After he looked up and saw that it was me, he slid his hands down his face and looked to his right so that he could look me in my eyes. His soul looked empty and gave the energy that there wasn't ever any coming back from this. Turtle then shook his head and put his face back into the palm of his hands.

I proceeded to walk upstairs, and as soon as I took the last step, I looked to my left about to go into my room. My eyes were immediately turned to Nigel's room. An image of his lifeless body lying on the floor popped in my mind. I screamed to the top of my lungs then everyone started to cry in a sequence.

That's one moment that I'll never forget because it was so quiet that you could hear a pen drop until I screamed. Reality set in that everyone was downstairs. My house was full but to me, as I was walking upstairs my home felt completely empty. A thought came thrusting through my mind, "Mika, if you don't hold it together, nobody else is going to hold it together." At that moment, I knew I had to be strong.

Later that night, I took a shower and cried an immense amount of tears. The shower would then be labeled as the place where I'd go to release. As I stand in the shower feeling closed in and under the water, I am free to cry, scream, and yell. Afterwards, I can wash all of the residue away. It's safe to say that it's my comfort zone. When it was time for me to go to bed, I could barely sleep; I tossed and turned all night. Turtle sat at the foot of my bed worried about how I was going to make it because truth be told, me, him, and Nigel had a conversation about the effects of suicide. After that conversation, Nigel started medication.

There are still parts of me that wonders if his regimen plan played a part in suicidal ideation because he was so young. I feel like his brain wasn't mature enough to have those types of thoughts. After Nigel's death, I felt like suing the manufacturer and the psychiatrist, but I wasn't strong enough to withstand that battle. It would have been far too draining due to the fact that they have so much money and God knows how many attorneys. I felt like I would be fighting for the rest of my life, and I didn't want to go that far.

The next morning, I walked downstairs to life already happening. For those of you who may not know, let me just inform you. The Black Culture does things a little differently when someone in the family dies—people inside and outside of your family start bringing food, drinks, and ask what you need during your time of bereavement. Well, for me, my siblings were in my home cooking and trying to bring life into a dead situation.

My first thought was, I have to call Nigel's school and tell them that he's no longer with us. Sighs. After a few rings, the secretary answered, "Huntsville High."

Me: May I speak with your principal?

Secretary: Hold one moment for me, please.

Principal Ashley: Hello, may I help you?

Me: Hello, this is Nigel Shelby's mother.

Principal Ashley: I'm hoping it's not true.

Me: It is.

Principal Ashley ended the call abruptly. Next thing I know, she's knocking at my door. Sarcastically thinking, she's his principal, she cares, Mika so of course she's going to drop everything and run to your house. Allow her to come inside.

Principal Ashley walked through the door and proceeded to take a seat on my couch. She held me when I cried, told me how much of a joy Nigel was, how Huntsville High was behind me 100 percent, and how they would be there when I needed anything. Of course, because everyone loved Nigel. Everyone had a NEED for Nigel.

Little did I know that I was sitting next to a woman who didn't understand the mind of a 15-year-old who was suffering from depression, anxiety, sexuality battles, and just being in a world that was created to tear him down. Ashley didn't understand what was happening, but I'm going to embrace this pale lady who sits before me and cares so deeply for my son. Since condolences have been expressed, it is now time for Principal Ashley to get back to the school. After about an hour, I telephoned Huntsville High School once more with hopes of speaking to Nigel's best friends, Jayda and Lena to retrieve Nigel's passcode to his phone. My mind was discombobulated so I didn't remember it.

Me: "Ma'am, is it possible for you to call Nigel's best friends to the office so I can see if they know his passcode ?

Principal Ashley: "Nobody knows the passcode to his phone, but I did want to tell you that there is a suicide letter in Nigel's book bag."

Me: "Ok, thank you!" I hung up the phone and immediately looked for Keta.

"Keta. Where's Nigel's book bag?" Keta walked upstairs to get his book bag.

After going through it, we found the suicide letter. Not one moment did it dawn on me to ask the administrator how she knew about a letter in my son's backpack. So yeah, here I am trying to process my son's death, while thinking, I must inform the rest of my family members that Nigel is deceased. *sighs* Social media is the solution.

I logged into my Facebook account and posted the news about Nigel's death. Of course, it was heartfelt. From what I read in the letter that Nigel left, he found comfort in his Instagram friends. I don't want to call his letter that he left a suicide letter because it didn't speak that. To me, a suicide letter lets someone know that you're about to end your life. Nigel didn't just do that.

First, Nigel wrote his best friend a letter telling her how beautiful she was and how much he wanted her to hold on and not give up. I made sure she got the letter.

For two, he gave me directions as to what he wanted me to do going forward. "Mama, I need you to stay strong, my passcode to my phone is ******, go on my Instagram and make this final post."

Nigel wrote everything that I needed to know in a journal. Even the answers that I was calling the school for. The letter that was in his book bag was in fact a suicide letter, but Nigel had a journal that I had to search for. It is so scary to let you all in about how deep Nigel's death was, but I'm going to continue.

Page one, Mama, my password to my phone is ******." Page two, "Can you Instagram all of my friends and tell them that I love them and thank them for loving me."

That last instruction was the reason that I posted to his Instagram. I had people ask me what my reasoning was for posting on Nigel's page. I never went into details, but I simply told them that it's what my baby wanted. I don't know if they knew that I was being 100 percent truthful or not, but he left instructions for me. I honored his last will and testament.

When people write their last will and testament, legally you are bound to honor their request(s). I did not know that the post on Instagram was about to open this whole door to Pandora's Box that I didn't even know existed.

Instantly, hashtag #JusticeForNigel went viral. It scared me 'cause what do y'all mean Justice For Nigel? I literally contacted several of Nigel's peers by Instagram direct message and asked, "Can y'all please take down this Justice for Nigel Page because he killed himself? There's no need for justice." At least that's what I was thinking at the time. However, anything in God's will, it will be done.

This is still day two after Nigel's death. Suddenly, my sister Lily called my phone and said, "Mika, there are a hundred kids at the playground by yo' house. It's something about a candlelight for Nigel."

"Go down there and tell them to walk down here."

After I hung up from Lily, my phone began to ring with people being concerned about me not informing them of the vigil. Hell, I didn't know myself as y'all can see. I finally walked outside and through the field and oh my gosh! All I saw was so many children. I was in tears after walking into this.

After getting to the bottom of things, I found that they set this event up via social media. I then told them that they may as well come on to my house. I have footage from that day. My Sister Lily had a pastor to travel from Florence to pray over everyone at the event. The children spelled out Nigel's name with candles, and it was the most uplifting thing.

During the process of all of this, keep in mind that my phone is ringing off the hook.

The internet was going wild! My son's story was spreading like a wildfire. I still don't understand why though. His peers and their parents created all this energy because they knew what was going on behind the scenes. I didn't know.

My phone rang and there was a lady on the other end of the phone. She said, "Hi, Ms. Shelby. I know you don't know me, but I'm stationed in Florida. I'm contacting you 'cause my phone is ringing off the hook. I work for Brandon Chisahm—you ever heard of him?"

"You talking about the man who represented the high profile case in Florida, some years ago," I asked?

"Yes"

"Ok."

"I work for him, and your son's story has been going viral. I saw your son's story on the internet and passed over it. But what got my attention was the fact that people keep calling my office telling me that I need to represent you."

I said, "Ma'am, I have no idea what you're going to represent me for, but I just want to concentrate on burying my son. I'm starting to hear all this negative stuff, and it's overwhelming. Right now, I just want to focus on burying my son. I'll contact you after."

"Ok, she responded."

Sighs Here it is something else for me to have to think about. What the hell is going on? Keep in mind that there are hundreds of people outside. This one girl walked up to me and said, "I'm on the phone with Big Money Undefeated Boxers people."

Wait, what?

She clarified, "I'm on the phone with an Undefeated Boxer's people and they want to know what they can do to help."

I'm overwhelmed as fuck. This is a bit much. I don't know what I need yet.

"It's ok, just calm down and give me your cashapp."

"I don't have a cashapp."

"Ok, first thing we have to do is make you a cashapp."

We created a cashapp that was linked to my number. Now, all these people are bombarding me with microphones and questions.

The chatters begin, "This is ABC News, this is NBC News—we want to speak to you about your son!"

I told the reporters, "Go away! I am not speaking with any of you!"

Oh my gosh! This is too much, but I thought, Mika, you must address the press. I walked over to my mom and said, "Mama, I need to address the press."

My mom replied, "Okay, baby."

She contacted a resource that she had at 48 News and told them that they needed to come to my home and do an exclusive on Nigel's death. The reporter did not hesitate to come out to my home on day three. Yes, I said three because I had to gather my thoughts and get comfortable.

After I completed the exclusive interview with 48 News, I got word that a reporter that I sent away tried to do some shady shit. The reporter printed a story that basically said that Nigel being bullied was bull shit and that it was a lie. I proceeded to call that news station and said, "If y'all don't pull that motherfucking story down right now, I'm going to sue y'all."

They proceeded to say the most shocking thing ever. It was stated that one of my family members told them that I was lying, and that Nigel was never bullied. It gets crazier. The family member who they named in the article wasn't kin to me. I couldn't believe someone would do that when my son wasn't buried yet. Where were their morals? Nonetheless, the story was removed expeditiously.

The rest of my weekend was a total blur, but I do remember being around everyone. People were constantly showing up at my house and that alone was too much for me. I remember feeling like I couldn't wait until the funeral was over so that they could leave.

Before this incident, me and Nigel were basically in our own little world. We would deal with people when it was necessary. For example, if there wasn't a family event going on, chances are, we are doing our own thing. But until this is over, I must deal with it.

As soon as my feet hit the floor on Monday morning, I prepared myself to go to the funeral home. Of course, I was still feeling like I'm a mom, so I need to be on my shit for my child. Keta and my mom drove me to the funeral home and stayed by my side while I had to do something that I'd never imagined doing. And definitely not so soon. We drove up and stood outside of the funeral home door while the funeral home associate unlocked the door for their daily operations. *Deep sighs* I thought, go ahead and walk in, Mika. It's time to plan this funeral.

I had maybe $1600 in the bank that was left over from my tax refund. Yeah, $1600 is all I had to bury my child. I sat down in a nice and comfortable seat at the funeral home and the associate asked, "What do you want to do? I have a book—we can talk about some different things."

I replied, "Since he is a kid, I don't want it to be like an old boring, grown person ass funeral. I want it to be a celebration of life because he was a child."

She said, "Well what are you thinking?"

"Balloon release"

She said, "You wanna release butterflies?"

"Yep!"

"You wanna release doves too?"

"Yep!"

"What kind of casket?

"Colorful. Rainbows."

"Let me show you some designs."

I flipped through the catalog and said, "Yeah, these are nice but none of them work. I would like his name, Nigel on it, rainbows, and with pretty colors."

"Ok, what else," she asked?

"Horses and a carriage."

My mama and Keta were sitting beside me with facial expressions that spoke, "Bitch, you're asking for all this shit. How In the fuck are you finna pay for this shit?"

Hell, I don't know, but it's what I want. Get it! We'll figure out how to pay for it later. The associate came back into the office with a printout of the bill, and we were already at $30,000 without a headstone included. Whew. I don't know how I'm going to pay for this shit.

On the brighter side, my cousin Elise started a GoFundMe Account that had been up for about an hour or two. It was already at about $5,000 so let's just up the limit to $26,000 so I can pay for all this elegant shit I just asked for. I don't know if it's gonna happen but we're about to see.

I didn't have access to the GoFundMe Account in the beginning, but I retrieved the information from Elise so that I could be in control. Here we go. I increased the limit to $15,000 the first time. Then, the funeral associate called and told me how much the headstone was going to be, so I increased it by another $10,000. I didn't need the people to pay for the entire invoice because Nigel already had an insurance policy of $5,000. The moment that I increased the limit to $25,000–he who shall remain nameless, logged into GoFundMe and donated $13,000. My God. His generous donation instantly put me at $26,000. The donations did not stop.

By the time I shut the GoFundMe down, it had a balance of $49,000. I had to shut it down because the numbers were scaring me. Nigel's funeral expenses were less than what was in the account. That was such a blessing to and for me because I knew I couldn't stay in my apartment. Plus, my job called me three days after I lost my son and said, "We know you're grieving but can you please come back to work?"

I haven't even buried my child and y'all calling me to come back to work? So yes, I needed the extra money. And because God is an awesome God and He has plans for me, I received a phone call from a woman.

"Hi, Ms. Shelby. How are you," she asked.

"I'm good," I replied.

"So, we know you have a GoFundMe Account started but I wanna ask you, how much is the total cost of the funeral?"

"Who is this?"

"I don't know if you ever heard of me, but my name is Laura and I own a vegan restaurant in Atlanta that's really popular."

"Well, hi, Laura."

"We want to help you. Can you send me your address? I'm about to pull up."

"Girl, quit playing!"

Y'all, she pulled the fuck up at my house like she's been knowing me all my life. But that's nothing. Just wait until the story progresses.

Laura and I sat down and talked. After getting acquainted she asked, "So how much is the funeral?"

"It's $30,000," I responded.

"What funeral home got him?"

"Serenity Funeral Home."

"Ok, I'm going to contact some people then I'll give you a call once things are settled."

We talked for a little while longer before she left to go back to Atlanta.

After she left and called me back, she said, "Camika, the funeral has been paid in full!"

Knocked off my feet and totally in shock, I asked, "Huh?"

She said, "Do you know the famous couple Gloria and Ben Washington?"

I answered, "Yes."

"You know that they have a Trans-daughter, right?"

"Yeah."

Laura said, "They wanna help you."

"I ain't never had nobody to do nothing for me before," I responded.

"Baby, when somebody wants to help you. Let them help you."

"Okay."

"Did you pick out the tombstone?"

"I picked out two of them. One of them was cheap and the other one was almost $5,000."

"Call up there and tell them which one you want."

Of course, I wanted the one that's $5,000 so I called and told them. The funeral home associate called back and said, "They called up here and paid for the entire funeral and tombstone."

I responded, "You got her to pay all except $5000, right? Because I have insurance."

She answered, "Yes, they paid $27,000 over the phone."

With that being said, I had $49,000 from the GoFundMe account for my pockets. Oh my gosh! I'm freaking the fuck out at this point. These people just gave me $50,000 and paid for my baby's funeral. I wish I could tell y'all all the people who made this possible, but I'll just say that the streaming network owner, a NBA player, a rapper, a singer, an actress, a retired NBA player, a restaurant owner, and every individual who donated to the GoFundMe Account have blessed me tremendously.

Before I continue, allow me to just wallow in the fact that the restaurant owner, Laura orchestrated all of this. She came and sat on my couch and laughed with me. I initially thought that she was gay because she wanted to help my son, but she's not! This lady is engaged to a man who is also a heavy hitting restaurant owner in Atlanta. My God. That was only God. Laura assured me that she'd be seated on the front row at my baby's funeral, and SHE WAS!

The celebrities continued to show their support for Nigel on Instagram. My baby was more obsessed with Ariana Grande than I am with Nicki Minaj. Everyone who knows me, knows that I love me some Nicki. I have literally put family members out of my house for disrespecting her. You're just not about to disrespect Onika Tanya Maraj around me. But anyway, my son loved Ariana just the same. And guess what, Ariana Grande shouted my baby out on Instagram.

Y'all, I have a face full of tears and a crack voice as I say this…Out of all the blessings and all the acknowledgements, that's the thing that has meant the most to me because my baby loved her. He used to give me quizzes: "Mama, when is Ariana Grande's birthday? Mama, what's Ariana's sign? Mama, did you know Ariana said this?"

Like, OH MY GOSH! That's just how he was when it came to her.

Our favorite song by Ariana was "Seven Rings." Me and Nigel would get in the car so crunk. He loved her. I was taking Nigel and my niece Summer 2019 to see Ariana and we never got to go, but I have the screenshot of her shoutout. I'll never forget that moment for Nigel.

This has been a chaotic time for me, but we are progressing towards the time of Nigel's funeral. Since the expenses of the actual funeral were paid, I needed to secure a venue.

I had to search for a place to have my baby's funeral because of all the people who wanted to come and pay respect to Nigel. I'm talking about the mayor, Laura, and many other people. So yeah, because my baby was getting much attention, I located a mega church in Huntsville, Alabama. This church was homophobic as hell from what I had been told. But because my baby's funeral brought so much attention, they OFFERED to have my son's funeral at their church house free of charge. Before I accepted their offer, I had to make some things clear.

I remember saying and thanking, " I know y'all are against gay people, and my son is gay. So, if y'all are wanting me to have his funeral at the church, just know I'm finna paint y'all church in rainbow."

Everybody who I'd been lining up and confirming to be on Nigel's program was a part of the LGBTQ Community. I needed the funeral to speak RAINBOW. Without hesitation, everyone agreed, and the church didn't have a problem. Thank God.

People were contacting me from the United Kingdom, wanting to know who my baby was. Nigel's name was on the Verizon building in New York. Like…I'm just trying to process all of this. The first days were bittersweet and heartwarming because Nigel's story was viral and touching so many people. In all of that, it was so sad too because Nigel wanted to be famous. I can only take it all in–because it was actually happening, and he wasn't here to see it. Yeah, this is a bit much for me. Overwhelmed was an understatement.

While I felt like I didn't want to deal with any more stressors, my dad came to talk to me about one of the major stress factors in life since before Nigel's birth. P. He wanted me to let him know that Nigel passed away. My father would not let up on me.

One day he said, "Mika, do not bury that child and not find his daddy. Don't do that to him."

So yeah, because of my dad being so forceful, I had to put in effort to find this ni**a! My intuition told me to do an inmate search on the internet because it had been months since we'd seen him. BINGO! I found that he was in prison again. *Deep sighs*

I called the prison and said to the operator, "My name is Camika Shelby and my son's father is incarcerated there. My son passed away and I need to speak to his father. Or can y'all tell him?"

The operator responded, "No, we'll let you tell him—he needs to hear that from you."

The guards went to get P from the cell–where he was located, and took him to the Warden's office to call me back. He obviously knew something was going on because there's no way that they're about to bring you into the office for a personal phone call.

P: "Hello."

Mika: "P, this Mika. Nigel is gone."

P: "Gone?"

Mika: "P, Nigel killed himself."

There was an awkward silence while holding the phone. What was only a few seconds seemed to be hours.

Mika: "P, you ok?"

Peso: "Nah… Nah… Nah…"

Mika: "They told me that I could tell you. I don't know what to say, but if you want to come to the funeral, I'll pay for you to come."

P: "Okay."

Our call ended.

I called the Warden's office a couple of days later and was prepared to pay for them to bring P to the funeral. The warden said, "He said that he doesn't want to come."

Just when I thought that P would finally show up, hmph—no show. I became offended as fuck because I offered for you to be here one last time for your son. What type of shit is this? I hate this ni**a. This is the last time you can see this child above ground and he doesn't even want to come. What the fuck is that to do? This nigga didn't even want to come to his own son's funeral, but he wanted to shake me down for money from a lawsuit. The FUCK!!!

THE LAST RIDE

April 27, 2019. It's my baby sister Kodie's birthday. My son's suicide happened on my baby brother's birthday, and we're burying my son on my baby sister's birthday. Their birthdays are forever tied to Nigel's suicide date and his burial date. I'm sure that my sister and brother have a hard time each year that their birthdays come. That's a hell of an event to have to share your birthday with. At times, I wonder if they feel how I feel.

The day of the funeral would be my first experience with Post Traumatic Stress Disorder (PTSD)—in the form of anxiety that I didn't know I had, and neither did I know what it was. I've always thought, what the fuck is anxiety? Stupidity. Why do we look down on what we don't know? Why do we try to tell people about something that we don't have a clue about?

In our culture, anxiety is not a thing, being stressed out is not a thing, and seeing a therapist is not a thing. Had I been educated about mental health a long time ago, I wouldn't have made a lot of choices that I've made in my life. Not knowing that I wasn't mentally healthy enough to make those decisions. These disorders were really relevant to me.

So yeah. Here I am—dressed in a black dress, a black wig with an array of highlighted colors, and my makeup done nicely. All I could think to myself was, Who in the hell wants to bury their child? Who wants to be called pretty? Hell, I feel like shit. I feel dead. Let's just do this shit and get this shit over with. On top of all of this, Nigel's sperm donor's family from California is here acting as if they knew my son.

My mom told me that his sperm donor's family wanted to know who was riding in the family cars. My baby didn't know y'all. Oh, excuse me, "Cameron" didn't know who the fuck y'all were. Yeah, I said Cameron. Those people gave my baby a whole other name when he was born. Nigel's grandmother would send Christmas cards addressed to Cameron. Who the fuck is Cameron? His name is Nigel Ahmad Shelby, but the cards would have Cameron Leshon Cruz on them—the name that P wanted to name him.

I agreed with Nigel's sperm donor that we could name Nigel Cameron L. Cruz if he was present during labor. Since he wasn't present, the agreement was null and void. So yeah, "Cameron" is nonexistent, and THE FAMILY are in the family cars so get in line when you can pull in.

But anyway…

I started to feel like I was having a heart attack. In my mind, I was about to die. I couldn't breathe, my chest was so heavy, my heart was racing, I couldn't walk down the stairs, and I stopped the procession of the funeral from moving forward. The first car in the lineup couldn't move because I was still upstairs experiencing what I now know as a panic/ anxiety attack.

As always, Keta was right beside me. Anxiously speaking, "Keta, I can't move. I can't breathe—something is wrong."

Keta calmly said, "you're having anxiety. Sit down and take slow deep breaths. It's going to be okay."

The softness of Keta's voice is soothing to my soul. I don't know if it's because she's my big sister or what, but her voice tends to calm me down. While talking to Keta, my body started to settle and I began talking to myself.

"Ok, you have to go. You have to do this. This is your child. You got to be there, Mika."

I finally gathered enough courage to walk downstairs. Once I walked outside, everyone was standing outside of their cars waiting for me. I proceeded to walk to the black stretched limousine that was reserved for me to ride in. I can remember seeing Turtle sitting in the car, but everything else was foggy.

While sitting in the funeral, my niece's mom sang a song but I don't remember her singing. The funeral seemed as if it lasted hours and hours and hours, but that was only an illusion. However, I do remember a lady singing, "Order My Steps."

I kept myself together until that lady opened her mouth to sing that song. I literally felt my soul leave my body—I lost it. I couldn't handle the anointing of her voice. It was so powerful and soul attracting. In that moment, her voice made me realize that I was burying my son. My sad reality had finally come, and I instantly broke down crying.

On my way out of the church, they were trying to calm me down and couldn't. It was only until my sister Lily yelled, "DELETE IT NOW! THAT IS SO DISRESPECTFUL!"

Somebody's child in my family was recording me as I was breaking down. After Lily snapped, I held myself together. Leaving that church was heavy. None of it made sense to me. Like, come on, this is Nigel's funeral we're having.

Yes, we're talking about the light of our family. The one who the family loved so much because we didn't think I could ever have children. You mean to tell me that we're burying this kid? This shit is not fair, it's not right, it's heartbreaking, it's soul breaking, and it's breathtaking. This shit ain't right, but here I am riding to put my son in the ground.

I feel empty. I feel low. I feel confused. I'm hurt—so many different emotions, but I gotta do this.

Turning on memorial parkway, I watched all of the cars that weren't a part of the procession stop as we came by. The police motorcycles sped past us to clear the traffic. As I was staring out of the window seeing the people watching this procession pass by, I wondered, Do they know that this is Nigel back here?

For those of you who don't know, in certain areas of the world, it is the nature of one to pull over on the side of the road when a line of funeral cars are coming through. That is the way that we show our respect to the bereaved ones and give them the right of way.

And here we are, having to go down this entire parkway to bury my son—from the south end to the north end. The ride to Meridianville was at least 20 minutes long from the church where we had Nigel's funeral. I wanted to bury him next to my grandma who'd passed away two months before Nigel's suicide.

We'd finally come to a stop in the middle of the road. What the hell is going on? Surely, we're stopping for a reason. The horse and carriage is coming. My God.

Of course the horse would be too tired to carry Nigel from the church so they met us at over the halfway mark of the parkway. With completely stopped traffic on both ends, the funeral directors transferred Nigel from the hurst to the horse and carriage. At that moment, I started to feel proud because it was such a beautiful horse and carriage that they found for my baby.

The director then walked to the car, opened my door, and said, "Ms. Shelby get out."

"Why," I asked?

"You're going to ride with your baby," the director said, while smiling.

Wow! Our last ride was with a horse and carriage. It was so special. The horse was dark brown with the prettiest hair; the carriage was black with glass and a red outline on it. It was beautiful. That alone was enough to brighten up my spirit. I went from crying and being sad to smiling and not being able to stop cheering because that last ride meant so much to me. It took me by total surprise—I didn't know that they were going to do that.

When I look back at the videos of me and Nigel coming up the parkway on the horse and carriage, it's hard to tell that I was burying my son. My face had just that much joy on it. It's simply because that LAST RIDE meant that much to me. I needed that time alone with Nigel–just one last time before I had to leave my baby in the dirt. *sighs*

As we were turning into the gate, we made a right turn in order to go around the circle to come up on Nigel's plot—which was on the left. Finally arriving, our family, friends, and others were there chanting, "LONG-LIVE-NIGEL and HYPE-ME-UP!" I felt so proud and honored that my baby brought the happiness out of people. I loved every moment of it until my reality settled in. Like, this is really the final goodbye.

I thought to myself over and over again, Just hold it together, God got you. Just hold it together, Mika.

I looked around and noticed that my grandmother didn't have a headstone at the time so there is another thought that's added. I needed to buy my grandma a headstone with some of the money that I received from the GoFundMe account. Although my mom didn't allow me to buy it, that was a thought at the time.

As the funeral directors were carrying Nigel to his final resting place, I sat on the front row admiring how beautiful his casket was. It was indeed pretty, but it was fucked up that my son was inside of it at 15 years old. What did we do to deserve this? Why would he do this?

Nigel, why would you do this, baby? You know you were my everything. I can't handle this so I'm going to just go ahead and buy the plot beside him. After we bury Nigel, I'm going to use the money to bury myself. I can't continue without this child. How am I supposed to do this? How am I supposed to eat, sleep, and breathe without this child?

It has been about this child for 15 years and now he's just gone. He was just here and now he's gone. God, why are you doing this to me?

Me and my child had taken a picture two months prior to his burial, in the same spot that he was being buried in. This shit is sick!

So yeah, here we are sitting here looking at a colorful ass casket with Nigel's body in it. This shit still doesn't make sense, but I'm gonna sit here and do it. I have to be dreaming because this doesn't feel like reality. I'm really having a long ass dream that I'm waiting to wake up from at any moment. When I wake up, Nigel will be here.

Nah, baby girl. This isn't a dream. You're not waking up from this. Nigel isn't getting up. He's not coming home.

It is now time for us to say a prayer and release these balloons, doves, and pretty little butterflies. After releasing the balloons, my balloons didn't go anywhere—they got stuck in a tree. I took that as a sign that Nigel wasn't letting go 'cause I wasn't ready. Everyone else's balloons floated away in the sky.

I'm such a spiritual person–so, I knew that it was about to be a process ahead of me. I try to find the signs in everything. Sometimes it may be a little paranoid-ish, but most of the time, there are lessons in the signs if I look deeply.

The butterflies were inside of this white envelope. When you opened it, they'd release. They were so pretty and colorful when flying out into nature. Finally, we released the doves.

I held it together while at the burial, but that feeling that I had seeing them roll my baby in the ground was a very sick feeling. I felt like I wanted to throw up the further that they rolled him into the ground. They were burying Nigel and didn't know that they were burying me too.

It was a bad thing, but it was a good thing. It was a bad thing because a part of me died with Nigel. It was a good thing because I was about to be born again. As I continue to point out the bad things in this story, be prepared for me to point out the good.

My family, Turtle, Team Nigel, and many others were there holding me up with support. I couldn't just fall. After Nigel was finally in his resting place, they couldn't cover him with dirt because it was too wet due to the previous showers of rain.

I took my balloons, getting stuck in the tree for what it was, and after putting Nigel's physical body in the ground, I said, "Come on Nigel. Let's go."

People used to think that I was losing my mind, but they really didn't understand that it was a way for me to grieve. I mingled with people after the burial, but I can't recall who because of the fog that I experienced.

The funeral is finally over and the hard part starts!

WHAT'S GOING ON?

My child is not in this car with me. He is not in his room laying in his bed, not in the shower, not singing Ariana Grande, not asking me a thousand questions, and not calling me bruh. Like… He's really not here anymore. How in the hell do I function when everything that I lived and stood for—my whole existence and reason for living…My child…My child isn't here. As a parent you wake up with the thought of feeding your child(ren), clothing them, and taking care of them. Your whole life involves your kids. For that to be taken away from you is enough but by the choice of your own child is a mind fuck. At this moment, I'm starting to process what the fuck just happened.

After staying in my apartment, the first night after Nigel's funeral, I knew I couldn't live there anymore. There was no way that I could keep walking up and down those stairs without having flashbacks of April 18, 2019, so I started packing everything. Since I'd just renewed my lease for my current apartment, I didn't know if my landlord would allow me to move. I went to talk to her about moving anyway. Thankfully, her and her team understood my circumstances and allowed me to break my lease. I moved into another two bedroom and two-bathroom apartment and set Nigel's room up the same way it was set up at our apartment he died in. At that moment, I knew I couldn't let him go yet.

I used the money from the GoFundMe account and paid my new lease up for two full years, bought me a cash Lexus, and gave the rest of the money away. I paid people's bills and gave them whatever else they needed. I felt like that was the biggest mistake I could've made.

After the money left, so did they. I would soon face some of my darkest moments alone.

These past four days have been foggy because of the limelight that was thrown at me. I'm confused because I've always wanted to be a star in this world. But the way that this shit is coming to me is crazy as fuck. Do I entertain this shit? Although I know that I may be able to help someone, I still questioned myself. Am I a bad mother to even want to go into the media world and speak about this situation?

My child hasn't been in the ground a full 24 hours yet and I have NBC, ABC, and more contacting me—wanting me to come sit down on their shows for interviews. Everyone wanted to know what was happening in my life. Hell, I don't know yet. I can't breathe.

Bitch you ain't got no time to breathe. You're going to do this or you ain't, I thought. Another part of me was saying, you need to process what the hell just happened. The last part of me was saying, you don't have time to process what has happened. If you're going to do something with this then you have to jump on this momentum right now 'cause someone may not care five months from now. You gotta do this while they care. Fuck it! I'm going in for Nigel.

Suddenly, a legal team member from Attorney Brandon Chisham's office persistently called me but I continuously brushed her off. I gave her the runaround because I didn't know what the hell was happening. Two weeks passed and I finally got the courage to stand. It's time to see what the fuck is going on 'cause major networks are calling me. Something is going on mama, and it's time for you to figure out what the fuck it is. I'm ready to talk.

Since the legal assistant was constant enough, she got my attention. It's finally time to address what she is talking about so I returned her phone call. She explained that there were several parents from Huntsville High contacting the firm about different situations that were going on inside of the school system. She led me to believe what happened to Nigel was the final straw to where everyone was ready to speak out.

After hearing her out, I thought, something may have not been right in my son's death.

The fact that I have this well known, heavy hitting attorney in the media's eyes wanting to represent my baby said something to me. I knew it was about to bring major attention.

Mika, are you ready for this? No, but what the hell else am I gon' do? I have to focus this energy somewhere because I can't just sit around and do nothing, I questioned and thought. Instantly, I was pushed into the limelight. Within no time after laying my baby to rest, I was thrusted into the mass media world– on radio stations, at news stations, at Alabama A&M speaking, in Birmingham, and at charity events in New York and Washington. It seemed as if I was everywhere—full speed. Absolutely no time to grieve or process Nigel's death. So, I definitely wasn't prepared for the opinions of social media

MEDIA TROLLS

It's about two weeks after Nigel's funeral and I'm all settled into my new apartment. Of course, Keta's by my side. She's never too far away. I'm sitting on my bed, scrolling through social media. At this point, Nigel's Instagram has reached over 100K followers and has received about five to six thousand direct messages. It was so overwhelming. I remember thinking, I can't respond to all of these people. There was a slew of messages from different reporters asking me to do interviews, and different organizations wanting me to come speak at events. Suddenly, I got the urge to just logout of Nigel's Instagram. I needed some time to process it all.

For some unknown reason, I didn't logout. Instead, I scrolled to one of his pictures and started to read the comments. Some of the comments were making me sick to my stomach. People were labeling me as a bad mom. They wrote that I didn't love my child. I didn't pay him any attention. The reason that he killed himself was because I treated him horribly. They also said that Nigel was neglected, and if he wasn't neglected, he wouldn't have ever taken his own life.

Where would these people get the notion that Nigel wasn't loved? Me and my family loved Nigel. Why would they think these things? I came to the conclusion that they were just a bunch of trolls—always wanting to have an opinion about someone else's life. Sometimes people use social media to make others miserable when they are. Why won't y'all understand that the shit y'all are saying is killing me? Don't y'all understand that I am a good mom? I always have been and always will be. I loved my son. I did not always make the best decisions, and I wasn't the perfect mom. I learned as I went as most do with their first child. There were times I'm sure that Nigel hated me or my parenting, but one thing for sure is–I never neglected him, I never turned my back on him, disowned him, and sure as hell never not loved him. Nigel was ALL ME, and since February 1, 2004, I had A Need For Nigel.

Although I know that I don't owe anyone an explanation, a part of me wanted to get on live and tell those people that Nigel meant everything to me. My family started telling me that I needed to stay off social media for a while. It was hard for me to do that because all of the pictures and posts of people showing Nigel love made me feel somewhat whole. That lasted a little while because when I thought about the negativity, it made me feel so much worse. In my heart I knew, if I was about to fight this fight, I needed to have thick skin.

From this day forward, I had to make a promise to myself, if you're going to continue pushing this movement, you have to have thick skin when it comes to social media and not be moved by the negativity, Mika. I made that promise to myself, but I'm not gonna lie, I cursed a couple of people out along the way. Sometimes trolls just go too far.

As hard as I tried not feeding into the nonsense on social media, there were some things that someone said that I'll never forget. I posted a video of Nigel, an asshole who had the nerve to comment, wrote, "Get over it already. His gay ass gone to hell."

What type of shit is that to say about a 15-year-old child–to a grieving mother? Who are you to say that my baby is gone to hell? Who are you to inflict pain on a person who you don't know? And you're bold as fuck to tell me to get over his death at two weeks after his death. That's just wicked. I felt like they went too far so I had to respond. Now, I am definitely a child of God, but that day, I became a messenger for Satan. It pissed me off to the point that I didn't act Godly at all that day.

I forgot what I said to them, but they got the hell off my page–fast. If I would have known or found out who that person was, I would've probably gone to jail. I'm pretty sure that they were just bored and wanting a reaction from me. Not knowing that saying some shit like that hurt me to my fucking soul.

When it came to me losing my baby, a lot of people tried me. Including my relatives. There were family members that I wanted to beat the fuck up, 'cause some of the things that were being said and done behind my baby's death were disrespectful. Sometimes I felt as if certain things were immoral 'cause I wouldn't have done or said the shit that they did. It took everything in me not to crash the fuck out. Somehow, I always allow the good part of me to lead the way. A part of me knew that there was a bigger purpose in this. I kept telling myself, just hold on Mika. For the most part, I've learned to kinda block them out because we live in a fucked up world. People can have all of the facts staring right in front of them, and they'll still go with their bull shit ass opinion. They would rather thrive from a lie than believe the truth. It's stupid, but again, that's the world we're living in. It's just so hurtful though when you experience such tragedy and those closest to you only support when it is beneficial to them.

A GRIEVING MOTHER

A Swiss American Psychiatrist by the name of Elizabeth Kubler-Ross is credited to the Five Stages of Grief: Denial, Anger, Bargaining, Depression, and Acceptance. For me, the anger and depression ran rampant.

I started to lose faith in God. I argued with Him for a very long time. I was mad as the fuck with God. I said to Him, "That is not what the hell I asked you for! When I said protect him, I DIDN'T MEAN FOR YOU TO TAKE HIM!"

For a long time, I didn't want to pray; I didn't want to talk to God. Simply because I went to Him and told Him to protect my baby, and on the same day, he took my baby from me. I'm angry as fuck at You, God! Why would you do that to me? Out of all people, why would You do that to me, God? But y'all know… I had to stop questioning my God. 'Cause what He doesn't do is make mistakes. But at that moment, I can be real enough and tell you all that I questioned Him. I was upset with Him.

As y'all can see, I didn't want to talk to Him. I was mad as hell! How dare ME come to You boldly before I go to work and when I come home, my baby is lifeless? That alone is enough to fuck a person spirit up.

God said, "I wanna see how deep is your faith in Me. How much do you trust me? You asked me to protect Nigel. Imma give him the best protection that I can, and that's to bring him home. Let's see if you can handle that. You asked me for something and I'm going to give it to you. It may not be the way that you asked, but I'm gon' give it to you ."

Before I continued on with my story, I looked over at my therapist, Dr. Zee to make sure she was still following. To my surprise, she noticed my pause and stated, "Camika, tell me about your experience with anxiety and PTSD"

I took a deep breath and started once again. I was going to the hospital telling the doctors and nurses that I was dying and that they were lying to me. I told them that everyone had a certain agenda to push. I didn't know what was going on. I'm black! We don't go to therapy; we don't have anxiety—what the fuck is that?

Girl, get your shit together 'cause we fall, but we get up, I thought.

At least that's what we're taught. But what we're not taught is that there are a lot of ways that you can get up. Sometimes your mental health needs more attention than self-talk to be able to function at its normal capacity.

I knew that if I wanted to turn Nigel's death into his legacy, I needed to become mentally healthy. Mika, baby it's time for you to take some medication although it's against everything that you stand for.

It took me a minute to agree on the psychiatrist medicating Nigel. Once I did, he committed suicide. I remember asking Nigel's psychiatrist, "Is my son going to be okay if I put him on this medication?"

She responded, "He's not going to be okay if you don't put him on it." She lied because he still wasn't okay. He killed himself a few months afterwards.

So, I decided that I would see a psychiatrist for an evaluation. I was so angry because it seemed as if she only wanted to medicate me. My child is dead and you want me to take this shit too? Bitch, fuck you! I'm not taking this shit.

That was my mind frame for the first couple weeks of my therapy sessions. And I had to go to therapy on a regular basis because everyone around me knew I was about to crash and hit rock bottom. I didn't know.

Luckily, after Nigel passed, there were some genuine people brought into my life who wanted to see me succeed—they forced me to see what I didn't see. They told me that I needed to get help first if I wanted to accomplish anything. They put forth an effort to help me see that I was losing my mind, but I didn't want to believe it.

Every time I attempted to sleep, I was feeling like I was dying. Anxiety had its hold on me. But what I learned was that it was a much stronger form of anxiety. I was experiencing PTSD. I would literally wake up gasping for air, like someone was killing me. It was bad. My brain was not functioning. I was on the verge of really crashing the fuck out.

I didn't know how to process not having Nigel around.

Regardless of how anyone felt, I didn't like that psychiatrist so after a few sessions, I knew I wasn't going back.

INVESTIGATION

Mentally, I was still having hard trouble processing what was happening, what happened, and what was yet to come. The investigation started immediately after I talked to the legal assistant and agreed that I wanted to move forward with an investigation. So, throughout the entire investigation of my son's death, I told my legal team that I only wanted to be contacted on a need to know basis. I didn't want to know the specifics of the case.

It seems like everyone hears the word lawsuit and automatically assumes that it's a bad thing, and that it's about money. I'm gon' play devil's advocate a little bit because at the end of the day, it is about money to a certain extent. And here's why. There are some people that you can't get through to until you hit their pockets. That's the only way to get their attention. So yeah, it is about money but it's NOT about money if I'm making any sense to y'all.

In the process of preparing for a lawsuit, someone told P that he was entitled to a portion of Nigel's estate per Alabama's state laws. But to be honest, I believe in my heart that in order to keep P from going against me for money, my attorney reached out to P and told him about the money. In turn, my legal team represented P as well. Y'all know I had questions about that so I asked. My attorney told me that the firm did not reach out to P, but they wanted to represent him so he wouldn't retain his own lawyer and fight against me. I agreed to it, however, P is so lowdown and his guilt started to settle on his conscience.

During our first conversation about the lawsuit, P said, "I know I haven't been there so I'm not going to fight you. Whatever you feel like you're going to give me, I'm ok with it."

I offered him 25 percent and he agreed to it. We signed the papers and got them notarized as soon as we came to the conclusion with our attorney present. Upon the completion of the notary, we both left the county clerk's office. Oddly, P went to the attorney's office and showed his ass the day before we were at the statute of limitation.

P aggressively said to our attorney, "I'm firing y'all because y'all have tricked me into signing for this 25 percent! I want more!"

Now, how in the hell did we fool you P? We agreed on a certain percentage. Those people asked us if we understood what we were signing. He obviously was directed to pull this bull shit. If we didn't sign those papers together that day, we weren't going to be able to move forward with the lawsuit.

P put on so bad to the point that I had to either give him what he wanted or throw the lawsuit out of court. Because of my son's story and what I needed to accomplish for Nigel was greater than my hate for P, I asked again, "What do you want from this, P?"

He responded, "33 and a third."

There wasn't any arguing done after our conversation; I simply honored his request. I kept thinking that my son's story was bigger than these uncomfortable moments. Throughout the entire process of the lawsuit, I was NEVER comfortable around Nigel's dad.

The point of filing a lawsuit was to hold everyone who wronged Nigel accountable, and this ni**a was the first one to wrong him. And y'all want me to sit here on national TV and act like it's all good. At the fucking press conference, I walked out because I wanted to smack P ass in front of the world. He was on live television dramatically crying and putting the fuck on, "Ahhh, Nigel was such a good child. He liked to dance. He liked to sing."

P literally quoted things that he heard me say in previous interviews. I have to laugh to keep from crying now.

All of my genuine caring and support for my son's dad bit me in my ass when it was all said and done. I never wanted P to show up financially; I wanted him to just be a part of Nigel's life, physically. He handled me roughly when it came to this lawsuit. The same motherfucker who has never bought my son a sock showed up when he found out that money was involved. His ass did not have to burden anything that I have had to burden since the birth of Nigel or the occurrence of his death.

I had to bear the rumors/ voices of the outside people. One particular TV show portrayed that my son grew up in poverty which played a vital role in his suicide. That was a fucking insult. If my son had ever grown up in poverty, he didn't know it. My son had the best of everything from the time he came out of my womb. That's one area that I never slacked.

It was to the point where when Nigel was a young boy, one of his daycare teachers called and asked, "Ms. Shelby, can you bring Nigel some more shoes because he said he's not going outside in his new J's."

I busted my ass and put myself in situations I would never have been in if I did not have to fend for Nigel. I even took penitentiary chances. I did all of that for mine! So yeah, for a motherfucker to mention me and my son living in poverty on national television—that shit ate me the fuck alive! I have a video of my son rapping about how his mama always had multiple cars, how she was a hustler, and has always gone far. My child knew his mama was a motherfucking go-getta. That alone gave me the strength to eat that shit and keep quiet about it and do what I needed to do for my child.

And now that it's over, ain't no more being quiet! With that being said, nah, I never needed shit from Nigel's dad. I was 21 years old with my Mercedes Benz paid for, four-bedroom house, and balling the fuck out of control until I turned 25.

At the age of 19, I met a man who I called a colleague in the beginning of this story, but to most of you, he would be called a sugar daddy. He was in his 50s with a trade bringing in $150K-$300K from January to May—during income tax season. And guess what? He was fond of little ol' me so you know my baby didn't want for shit. That man saw what I didn't see in myself at the time.

He said to me, "If you give me a chance, I'm gonna make people hate you!"

I was so intrigued by his words, not knowing what the hell was finna come behind them. In fact, he did just what he said he was going to do.

At age 25, you couldn't tell me shit! I was well established in the financial aspect of things. Mentally? I was in a fucked-up situation and didn't even know it. But with growth comes wisdom, and we'll get into all of that later.

Don't get me wrong, I had to work to get there. I learned the trade, I mastered the trade and I took off with it. Some would like to believe that my colleague/ sugar daddy was only giving me the money, but nah, I worked for it. I've always been smart, but people thought that just because I grew up in the hood and I lived life with a hood mentality—that's all I had to me. BUT, it's not. I am so many things.

First and foremost, I am Nigel's mom. That'll never be taken away from me. Underneath that mom hat lies, a hustler, a student, a teacher, and much more. You can take me to the hood and I'm going to survive. Or, you can take me to the White House and I'm going to adapt. I can be corporate, I can be ghetto, I can be ratchet, I can be bougie, I can be rich, and I can be poor. I can be it all but right now, I'm just Nigel's mom and that's what I'll stick to.

The day that we went forward with the lawsuit, a press conference aired live on national television. This was the first day that I heard the basics of the lawsuits which were filed. The reactions that the people saw were raw reactions of me hearing the things that happened to my child for the first time. The emotions—the hurt, the pain, the anger, and everything else that I was feeling was too much. I had to keep myself in a place where I could be sane and functioning healthy.

Yes, I received the lawsuit before we filed it, but it was 50 pages. By the time I finished the end of page 2, I was defeated. I couldn't read anymore. There were 48 pages of horror that I hadn't read before press time. And 'til this day, I still haven't read the suit in its entirety because it's too much for me.

Today, I'm ok at times because it's nothing but God how Nigel left this world. I found out that Nigel attempted to kill himself the day before but it didn't work. His friends had taken him to the office because Nigel had a cut on his wrist and a ring (a bruise from the belt) around his neck. I knew nothing about the ring, and it's starting to make sense now.

The school administration knew that Nigel tried to kill himself the day before he actually committed suicide. Those people did not attempt to contact me. I want to highlight the fact that Nigel's first attempt of suicide was NOT successful. It was only when I asked God for His protection that my baby tried a second time and was successful.

After hearing some of the things that were done to my son and going home to think about them, I had to dig deep into my heart and allow my heart to speak for me and make some sound decisions. In solitude, I found that the school system needed to put a better policy and procedures in place. Ones that catered to implicit bias, bullying, and how to handle children with suicidal ideation. They also need to be taught to have compassion or some sort of empathy when it comes to students that they may not understand or relate to.

Although I don't know each individual's heart who mistreated my baby, it's easier for me to process that the things that happened to Nigel in the school system were not from a cold-hearted place. But they were from a lack of knowledge. Yeah, it's easier for me if I process that the harm in which was done to Nigel was from a place of ignorance. I'd like to think that the things that were done to Nigel wasn't from a personal or evil place in their hearts. Who am I to say otherwise?

The lawsuit was heavy as fuck. I didn't want to put myself in a place where I was the judge of what happened to each irresponsible individual's fate. I'm not God. My mission for this lawsuit is to get the school board and the world to see that change needs to happen.

It was an extremely long road. Finding out the things that occurred in Nigel's last days of living makes me sad. There is so much room for improvement when it comes to being responsible for other peoples' children. And sometimes people are oblivious to the fact that they may not be right in certain situations. You may have not handled a situation in the proper way, and it's ok to admit that. I'm not judging anyone for the mistakes that they have made, but I'm going to hold them accountable so that these mistakes are not made again.

I feel as if I've always had pure intentions, but people were expecting for my intentions to be vengeful. There have been people asking me why I didn't have the children and parents arrested for bullying. I tried my hardest to get them to understand that hurting others was not what the lawsuit was about. For one, kids are going to be who they are. Kids bullied kids when I was in school. I've been bullied and I've been a bully. Yes, Nigel was being bullied, but the multitude of my reasons behind this lawsuit came from the school allowing those events to take place.

Not only did the administration not stop it, but they also played a part in it. They are responsible for our children for eight hours a day. If my son was being bullied while in their care, you're supposed to call me. As an administrator, your job is to pick up the phone and notify all involved children's parents. We should be aware of what's going on. Not only was it not reported, but there were allegedly incidents where it was instigated. I'll never know if it's true or not because we settled outside of court. If it is true, I'm not God so it's not up to me to hold them responsible for that. I only wanted change, not to discipline an adult. I wanted them to know that their actions weren't appropriate for this situation, so they all needed to learn multiple ways to act accordingly. God can do more than I can.

If the administration was educated about different ethnic and cultural backgrounds, some of the things that come off as being racist wouldn't be thought of as such. What gets through to Christy, may not get through to Randal. You must know that you can't use a technique on Randal if it's not going to work for him. You have to know how to help both of them and not just one of them.

Regardless of what technique the administrator thought she used and if she thought that it was right, my child is gone. He's no longer living. We were raised differently, and you may have thought that you haven't done anything wrong. I'm not judging you, but be open to new strategies. The way that you handled my son didn't turn out right. My child is gone, but I bless you and don't have any ill wills against you, Principal Ashley.

God chose Nigel for many reasons, but the most important reason to me was for the situation to teach me who I really am. I was blessed enough to bring a child into this world—gay or not gay. Nigel was a virgin. He never had sexual relations with anyone. You can't condemn him for a feeling that he never acted on. I said all of that to say this… God gave me a real live angel. He placed an angel inside of my womb and allowed me to bring him into this world.

It is my hope that one day I am able to receive what happened to my son so that I can process it in a healthy way and not with negative triggers. If I read it in these times, it's going to make me depressed, angry at myself, angry at the administration, and angry at the children who were involved. I don't want to deal with angry emotions. I know I need some healing—some REAL THERAPY, from a psychiatrist.

THE NEED FOR THERAPY

The first thing that you would think you'd see because of the saying "laying on a couch in my therapist office," was not there. I was expecting to see a couch. Instead, there were some hard ass green chairs with a wooded outline. Everything about this office screamed outdated, plain, and depressing.

So here I am, finally taking a seat to look at a second Psychiatrist's face because the first one was just a hell no for me. This lady had short, weird, frizzy brown hair—looking like she may have been stuck in an era that I wasn't born into. She was dressed in a white shirt that looked as if it was from a thrift store, plain ass khaki pants, and plain white shoes. Everything about her appearance was basic as fuck, but there was something about her smile that was warm and welcoming. Yet, irritating at the same time. I guess it was irritating because I didn't want to be sitting in her office.

She stared at me and asked, "Why are you here?"

I ignored her and proceeded to look around the room. There was an awkward silence in the room until I decided to break it.

Me: "I'm here 'cause people are telling me that I need to be."

Therapist: "Who are these people that you're speaking about," the therapist asked?

Me: "The people from the emergency room," I replied nonchalantly.

The therapist asked a lot of other questions that I didn't care to answer 'cause I'm black. We don't do this. We don't come to therapy and talk about problems outside of our household. We don't get medicated. This is not how I was raised, but I'm sitting in this chair because how I was raised isn't working for me.

I'm on the verge of losing my mind, I don't know if I see myself living past the next few weeks. Nigel's death has left such a darkness over me.

At any moment, I feel like I'm going to stop breathing. I'm really not sure at what moment I felt that being in therapy might help, but I do remember moments of feeling that I needed to try something, or I wasn't going to make it out.

The therapist decided to take another approach, so she said,

"Tell me about your childhood."

Me: "That's not why I'm here."

Therapist: "Well, tell me why you are here."

Me: "I am here because my 15-year-old son committed suicide, and everyone thinks that I'm losing my mind."

Therapist: "Are you losing your mind?"

Me: "I don't know!"

Therapist: "Do you feel like you're losing your mind?"

Me: "I feel like I'm losing myself."

Therapist: "What does losing yourself feel like?"

Me: "I don't want to go anywhere. I don't want to do anything. I have a boyfriend who has been in and out of my life for 15 plus years, and he's always upset because I don't want to participate in everyday things. I just don't wanna deal with the world."

Therapist: "So what happens when you try to deal with the world?"

Me: "I can't breathe. My chest is heavy. I feel like I'm having a heart attack."

Therapist: "So it sounds to me that you have severe anxiety. Are you open to being medicated to treat your anxiety? Because after tellin' me the numerous times you've had episodes, I feel that it's only going to go away if you're treated."

Me: "Lady, I'm not finna take any medication! You're sitting here telling me that I need to take the same medicine that I feel like played a role in my son's death."

Therapist: "I understand that Ms. Shelby but the medicine has different effects on adults than it does children.

I began crying after sitting in this hard ass chair feeling like a crazy person, and this lady is telling me that the only way that I can feel normal again is if I allow them to prescribe me some medicine. I've been to the emergency room several times before coming here. The doctors have prescribed me Xanax and all types of shit. I didn't take none of that shit, and now I'm sitting here feeling like it's the only choice that I have.

I'm just going to agree to this shit so I can leave this session, but I'm not going to take this shit for-real.

Me: "Ok, I'll take it."

Therapist: "I can't force you to take it, but if you give me a chance and work with me, I promise I can help you feel better."

Me: "Ok, I said I'll take it."

Therapist: "I'm going to write you a prescription for some Zoloft. Start the first few days taking a half of a pill. After the first three days, take a whole pill every day."

Me: "Yeah, whatever." She handed me my prescription and I snatched it from her hand and proceeded to walk out the door.

Therapist: "Ms. Shelby, don't forget to stop by and let them schedule your next appointment."

Me: "Yeah, Yeah, Yeah!"

I walked up to the checkout window and gave the receptionist the paperwork. She took the paperwork, typed some shit in the computer, scheduled my next appointment, and told me where to pick my prescription up. Afterwards, I stormed out of their office with an attitude.

Once I walked up to my 2018 White Malibu and sat in it for a few minutes, my heart started to race. I felt completely overwhelmed. Why am I having an anxiety attack outside of the office that's supposed to make me feel better? Really? In the parking lot though? What did I do to deserve this? How am I going to get through this? I proceeded to drive to get the prescription filled, but I didn't take the Zoloft.

HEAVEN SENT

I'd taken some time off from work because I was not able to function mentally. So, one day I sat home alone while my boyfriend Dre was at work. Dre I feel is truly the love of my life. Me and Dre have been running in and out of each other's life since Nigel was two. I had a special connection with Que but nothing like what I felt for Dre. With Que it was sweet and sensitive. With Dre, it's intense, it's never-ending, it's electric, it's unpredictable. It's so passionate, It's a true soul tie. This man has had a piece of my soul since the day I met him. No matter what road each of us travels, it always leads back to one another. Yeah, Dre does something to my heart that no other man has ever done, but honey, that's a different book for another time.

Shakes off memories of meeting Dre

My day started as any day normally would. One day at a time is all I'm thinking about.

Breakfast is my most favorite meal of the day, so I prepared it. I fried a few pieces of bacon, a piece of sausage, some scrambled eggs with cheese, and I baked some biscuits. After cooking, I ate and walked towards my bedroom. Before I proceeded to walk through my bedroom door, I stared inside of my room and looked at the placement of everything.

I had a queen size bed that was sitting to the right of the room, a dresser with a mirror on top of it, a nightstand at my bedside, and a TV in front of my bed—on a taller stand. I finally entered my room and sat on my bed with one leg on the bed and one leg off of the bed while rolling up a blunt. The music was already playing on my TV because I start my days by playing music. Music is good for my soul—especially anything Nicki Minaj.

For some reason, I could hear my heart beating to every beat of Nicki Minaj's song,"Pills N Potions" as it played loudly on my TV. I proceeded to fire a blunt up and take the first pull. Suddenly, my mind blacked out. It was an indescribable feeling, however I jumped up from the bed and ran to the kitchen for water.

I stood in the kitchen and downed the entire bottle of water, without taking a breath. The water did not help whatever was going on with me, but I unconsciously grabbed another one and opened it. Suddenly, I thought that I needed air.

Instead of running outside, I ran back into my bedroom and raised the window up really high and dropped to my knees. As all of this was occurring, my heart was thumping extremely hard. It felt as if my heart was about to burst through my chest. I immediately began to pray and plead to God, "God, I don't know what is happening right now but please don't take me out this way. Please don't. I got so much that I wanna accomplish. I need to figure out what happened to my son, God. Please don't take me out this way!"

Next, I called my boyfriend Dre's, phone yelling hysterically at him throughout our entire conversation, "I need you to come home now!"

He said, "What's wrong?"

"I don't know, but I'm about to call the ambulance! But just come home now!"

Of course, me calling and yelling at him the way that I did, and him not knowing what was happening, he panicked. At the time, we were experiencing a Global Coronavirus-19 (COVID-19) Pandemic and people were dying every day due to the virus. So anytime anyone got sick, the fear of a COVID-19 diagnosis was gut wrenching. My boyfriend instantly thought that I was meaning sickness in my body. He never thought that I was sick in my mind. Neither did I understand it at the time. I thought I was about to die.

My boyfriend arrived shortly after we ended our phone conversation. The door was unlocked for him, but he was scared to come inside.

"What if you have COVID? I don't want to catch it," he said.

"No, I promise you. This is not COVID; I feel like I'm about to have a heart attack," I responded.

He finally walked inside of the house. I stripped out all of my clothes, ran in my room and jumped in the shower. I felt as if the shower was the only thing standing between me and death. Dre walked inside of the bathroom and asked, "What can I do to make it better? What do you need me to do?"

"I don't know, call somebody! Call the ambulance! Call my mama," I yelled.

He proceeded to call my mom and attempted to explain what was going on. My mom said to him, "She's having an anxiety attack."

I can remember thinking to myself in that moment, She don't know what the fuck she's talking about. I'm about to have a fucking heart attack! What the fuck is anxiety? Please just call the fucking ambulance! My boyfriend finally hung up from my mom and called the ambulance.

I had to be standing in the shower every bit of 30 minutes before he decided to do so. To look in his eyes and see a 280 pound, 6 feet 4 inches black man defeated, defeated me. There was nothing I could do to help him because I couldn't help myself. For all I knew, I was about to die in that apartment. Dre and I were finally reunited 4 months after I lost Nigel. He left home 6 years prior and though we spoke over phone and social media a few times, that's really all it was. Neither one of us knew that losing Nigel and my mental health was about to put us through the greatest test of our relationship.

I thought, None of this shit that I want to accomplish in Nigel's name is gonna get done because his death is too much for me to deal with. The shower was the only thing that stabilized my breathing.

Suddenly, I heard the paramedics coming through the front door. Ok Mika, get out of the shower.

I removed my head from underneath the shower head of running water, stepped out of the tub, and wrapped a towel around me as the water was dripping from my hair and body.

The paramedic asked my boyfriend, "Where is Ms. Shelby?"

"Let me go get her."

My boyfriend came to the bathroom and said to me, "Bae, put some clothes on. The paramedics up there."

I got dressed and came out of my room. As I was walking down the hallway, I stared at a painting of Nigel and immediately felt like life was being drained from my body. By the time I walked through the living room and saw a female and a male medic, I dropped down on the couch. My body didn't have any more energy. I just kept thinking, I don't want to die God, but I know I'm about to.

The female medic placed the blood pressure cuff around my arm and checked my blood pressure. Alarmed, yet empathetically speaking, she said, "Your blood pressure is so high! I need you to calm down. I know you don't understand what you're going through right now, but you're having an anxiety attack…I suffer from anxiety. And listening to all of the symptoms that your boyfriend gave the dispatch, I knew exactly what was going on. And when I walked through your door and looked around…I knew exactly why…I am so sorry for your loss. I know this has to be the hardest thing, but I promise you, you can get through this. I have never experienced what you have gone through, but I do suffer from anxiety. And there have been days where I couldn't even get up and go to work because of my anxiety. So, I understand."

As I write these words with a face full of tears while reliving this moment, I know that she was heaven sent. Out of all of the medics in the world, God sent one who knew exactly what I was going through. As she was speaking to me, her voice was so soothing that I could feel my blood pressure decreasing. I could feel my breaths per minute slowing down. I could feel my heartbeat slowing down. Everything about her energy was just what I needed to calm down.

When she revealed to me that she got control of her anxiety by taking medicine, I knew in my heart that I had to take my prescribed anxiety medicine. From that day forward, I started medication and I never had to call the paramedics again.

It would be the little things that would break me from the feelings of not wanting to take the medicine. I would cry and plead to Nigel, I need you to come to me. And one day he finally came to me in a dream.

I asked him, "Nigel, what do you do when you're not with me?"

In the happiest and silliest voice, he said, "Mama, I be everywhere!"

That response was enough for me to feel somewhat free. That dream gave me the push I needed to not give up. From that dream, I also interpreted that he was letting me know that he was alright so he needed me to be alright.

So yeah, if I wanted to go forward with finding out if this lawsuit was really a lawsuit, or creating Nigel's legacy, I needed to be mentally together. Finally, I called and told my psychiatrist that I would take the medicine, and she was so happy. She was happy to the point where I felt in my heart that I was doing something right for once.

My son's incident spoke, Hell nah, you don't need to take this medicine.

Then again, I had to do my research. I now take the same medicine that Nigel was taking. The only difference is the medicine has a different effect on an adult's brain than it does a child's brain. A child's brain isn't developed fully so it's not able to function with all of this extra shit. They'll be led to believe that it's going to help them, but that's not always the outcome.

I'm quite sure that's the reason that suicide rates are higher in children who take antidepressants than they are in adults. I found this research on the internet before Nigel started Zoloft, and that's the reason that I didn't want to start him taking it. But his psychiatrist did a hell of a job convincing me. I would have done anything to save my child!

'Til this day, I don't know if it was genuine or if my psychiatrist was happy that she won–and I broke down and decided to take the medicine.

But what I do know is for two years, I've sat in this one place of comfort. I have felt that my mental health was in good hands since I left the office. Although I started the medication, I knew that there was a long road ahead of me. The loss of my baby, thinking of him, me never being a grandma, him never going to prom. I used to always say things like: When my baby gets his first car, I'm buying him a foreign car. I don't give a fuck about what nobody says. If his mama rides foreign, he rides foreign. *Sighs* None of that is ever going to be my reality. How in the hell do I swallow this pill? My baby was so handsome and talented. This is so unfair. I have this need for Nigel, and he's no longer here. I know that one of the instructions that he left for me was to "stay strong, and don't give up" but how do I do that?

Nonetheless, I have to follow his last will and testament.

BLOOD MONEY

We have now reached year 4 after Nigel's death. This shit has felt like such a drag. But…We are finally back in court for mediation—a day of tiresome arguing. All of it felt so weird. Why are we sitting here going back and forth about a child's life who committed suicide? A child who had so much to offer the world, turned into human beings putting a price on him after death. But ok, if this is what we have to do, let's roll with it.

It started off laughable, but it ended in a way that I was ok with. For me to continuously sit in an office and fight about money felt immoral. You mean to tell me that I have to sit in this room and go back and forth with y'all about a dollar amount that I think my child's life was worth? This shit is sickening, and it feels like blood money! Money that comes from a sacrifice. Money that you don't receive in a righteous way.

So no, it wasn't a good feeling at all. At that moment I felt like I wanted to donate all of the money to charity, but I quickly thought, Why should I do that when I can use it to share Nigel's story and keep his memories alive. That very thought made me feel as if I could wash the money. And the only way that I could do that is by investing it into something positive.

After 12 long and tiresome hours of negotiations, we reached two agreements. Of course I won't ever tell the world how much money I walked away with, but I will say that just because I settled for

$840,000, doesn't mean I left the table with that amount. There were attorney fees, and other legal fees and a percentage that I had to give my son's sperm donor—that he definitely didn't deserve, and other fees for filing the lawsuit.

Finally, something greater and worthy of my joy and inner peace came out of the settlement. The non monetary policies that they were putting in place to change the way the administration handled things when it comes to the LGBTQ children in their school district. Yes! Hopefully no one else's child will have to go through this.

At this point of my conversation with Dr. Zee, I felt like I'd given her enough for the day. I felt relieved and so overjoyed that I jumped up and said, "Girl, I'll see you another day!"

Y'all, I ran out of her office so fast and went home to process the verdict that was given during mediation.

A MESSAGE TO THE LGBTQ+
PARENTS & COMMUNITY

Settling out of court gave me more motivation to keep going. It gave me the thought that I was being heard and creating change. Before then, I was on a constant emotional roller coaster. Asking myself if I was doing what was right. Whether or not I can make it through these tough times, still sane.

I have been asked, what is it about my story that gives me the knowledge to give advice to the next parent when dealing with their child who's different, who's gay, not popular, or reserved. You know, a child that you wouldn't just consider what society labels as a normal child. It's because I've dealt with it and my son's story ended with him taking his own life. Because of this experience, I feel that I'm the perfect person to give advice and answer questions if I can about what to do and what not to do in similar situations. The best teacher is experience, and I've learned some of the greatest lessons through experience.

When your child is struggling, it's important that both parents are present. It's important that both parents connect. Don't get me wrong, I do understand that it's hard to coparent with someone who is a parent from an ego point of view instead of doing what's best for the child. I dealt with that for 15 years.

Nigel's sperm donor was very selfish and egotistical. He came around and buttered Nigel up with an image of love and a happy family whenever he'd show up. But because I didn't want to deal with his bull shit on a personal level, Nigel's sperm donor took it out on him by disappearing. Two people do not have to be best friends in order to be coparent. You both must be willing to put your child first. That's all it takes. When both parents focus on putting the child first, nothing else matters besides that child. So yeah, egos tend to be damaged.

I've seen Nigel's sperm donor three or four times throughout the entire legal process and that's because I had to be in his presence. Being around him and being able to spot his guilt instead of his grief, I can honestly say, the guilt of him neglecting his child is whooping his ass. But his ego is still there. He's still going to forever play the victim role. It's heartbreaking.

I be ready to whoop his ass every time I see him. On the strength of me putting Nigel first, I don't. I feel that as a parent, some things should come naturally. The love, the mindset, and the responsibilities that you must have to care for your child, doesn't always come naturally to everyone. Some never learn to be nurturing to their children when they need it. Some people learn it right off, but others find it when it's too late. If one just dared to think about it, what's life without your kids? I couldn't imagine not having some of the special moments that I had with Nigel.

Nigel, where's your report card? Nigel, did you do your homework? Mama, can I go outside with my friends?

It's the little shit that I yearn for. This seems so unfair. And as a mother, I've had hard lessons when it has come to parenting. The lessons from working a lot.

During times of Nigel's life, I worked two jobs so that he could have the things that he wanted in life. I have a job now and I've been off work more than I've worked. That shit doesn't mean anything to me. There was a time where I didn't give a fuck about bills. I didn't care about being evicted. I didn't care about my lights being cut off. I didn't care about anything because my baby was gone and never coming back.

So, when I hear about parents who are always at work trying to provide for their kids, what I'm thinking is, you're an idiot. You still think that shit matters, and it doesn't. Don't be like me and find out the hard way! My son was at home hanging himself while I was at work slaving for the bare minimum. None of that shit matters. Don't be like me. I had to lose my son to learn valuable lessons about parenting.

The most damaging thing that a parent can do to a child is silence them. A child shouldn't ever feel silent at home. If a child shall have any place to feel comfortable speaking, it should be at home. No matter what, it starts at home.

In black homes, we must stop the stigmas that we were raised on. I'm saying black homes because I can only speak about the culture that I was raised in. When an adult says something to you while you're a child, you can't speak back. You must just listen and take what they say. If you speak back, you're being disrespectful. That must stop! That example is the first thing that we do to silence our children.

We don't allow them to speak back. No, I'm not saying to allow your children to be disrespectful. I'm saying afford them the opportunity to tell you how they feel. Allow them the opportunity to try to get you to understand how they're feeling–regardless of the situation that you all are communicating about.

It's as simple as saying that you're preparing hamburgers for dinner, and they tell you that they want pizza. There's a reason that they want pizza. Even if you don't give them the pizza, allow them to explain why they want the pizza. This gives you an opportunity to understand who your child is.

A lot of children get lost because of generational curses. Listen to these kids. I'm telling you. You would hate to learn these lessons through burying your child. That's how I had to find out. It does something to my soul to see people take their kids for granted now. I can no longer have the simple things from my son. You have parents who say, "Ooo, this child is getting on my nerves. Calling my name and don't want shit!"

I'm on the other end thinking, you should be thankful for that simple blessing.

A lot of parents don't understand that their way can and oftentimes are made through their children. They are so much smarter than you, and most people don't want to acknowledge the fact. I feel that we should use that fact to help everybody up. Don't envy your child or be mad at that child for reasons that you shouldn't be. Accept that God gave you a child to help you be a little smarter. These children are growing up in a digital world–a world where we haven't been in long. So, a lot of things that they are born into is second nature to them–meaning, they can show us the easier way to navigate.

Parents should pay attention to their kids. Listen, my baby was spoiled; he had everything that he wanted. But when it all boils down, none of those things matter. I only miss my son's presence, his smile, his laugh, and his voice. I don't miss buying him shoes or paying the rent for him to sleep. Nigel mattered. I should've just bought him some shoes out the fucking dollar store and spent that time with him, 'cause that's what the fuck I can't get back. I view things differently now.

All this slaving to pay bills doesn't matter! I will stress this fact until the end. I could have been creating memories with my son instead of being at work. Don't get me wrong, I know that as parents, we must be providers. But, don't let your sole purpose of being a financial provider be the reason that you forget to provide what's important. The important things are love, time, conversations, and being in the presence of your children—doing nothing.

When it was time for me to bury my son, I didn't have to lift a finger to bury him. Y'all have already read how things happened, but I want to focus on the message from God. He was telling me that He didn't need me to focus on how I was going to pay for anything, because He already had people in place. He needed me to focus on laying Nigel to rest so that He could prepare me for a path that I had no idea I was about to embark on. Stop focusing on the money for once! I got you when it comes to that. I need you to focus on your mental health. I need you to focus on Nigel's legacy. I need you to focus on the reason I gave you Nigel in the first place.

I had to lose Nigel to learn that the things that I felt were valuable, weren't valuable at all.

As of a couple of weeks ago, I had officially become a woman of six figures. I'm still driving the same little dusty ass car I had. Still living in the same dusty ass apartment that I had. The old Mika wore nothing but labels and drove foreign cars. The old Mika laid in nothing but the best. But this new Mika? Oh, she knows that all that shit has no true value.

I've been torn apart since Nigel's death, with the decision to step into the limelight. I've heard that people say that it's evil that I'm always in the media behind Nigel's death. They say that I used my baby's death to come up in the world. I have even had an aunt say that I sacrificed my son. People have said that I was pushing the "gay agenda" on their children. They have said many things without fact, but allow me a turn to address my agenda.

As Nigel Shelby's mom, I'm pushing the "Support everyone for who they are" agenda. I'm pushing the "I loved my child regardless of who he loved" agenda. I'm pushing the, "If your child is gay, this is what you need to do to understand your child, so you don't lose them" agenda. I can't help that my son was gay; that's nothing that I chose for him. It's really nothing that he chose for himself because he was born that way, contrary to what anybody may believe. I'm pushing "The I loved Nigel Agenda!"

I hear all of you guys' comments, but I will not allow anyone to deter me from what I know I was given this opportunity to do.

When we all get in tune with ourselves, we realize that there is nothing in this world that is not going to be sacrificed. Every day you wake up is a sacrifice, and I understand that. With that being said, I'm going to continue to push Nigel's purpose. And whatever agenda that the people want to label it as, I'm gonna let them do it.

When I open the thousands of messages on Facebook, Instagram, Snapchat, and emails that I receive from parents and kids, I get a feeling of being whole. They have told me how much Nigel's story helped them. They've expressed how much my speaking and advocacy helps them by giving them the will to want to live.

So, all the negative things that people have to say can continue. 'Cause these people that I'm helping are finding life again that can't ever amount to any dollar amount. I lost my baby, but I gained so much more purpose. And for that, I'm gonna take it and run with it. 'Cause that's what Nigel would want me to do. My baby told me, "Mama, don't be sad, stay strong, and do what you gotta do." For that, that's what I'm gonna do.

I will leave y'all with this. My baby used to always tell me, "Mama, I'm gonna take care of you for the rest of your life." He never said that he was going to be here to do it. He's not present with me, but he's making sure that I'm taken care of. So yeah, there's a tragedy every second, but every second, that tragedy comes with a lesson, turmoil, or triumph. It's honestly up to you to choose what you make of it.

I knew that I wasn't going to allow Nigel's suicide to be the only way that people defined him. I knew that I wasn't going to allow Nigel's suicide to define me although that almost happened. It nearly took my will to live, but I had to fight those demons.

Throughout this entire process, I have had two grief counselors, three therapists, and three psychiatrists because I had to do trial and error to see who could meet my needs. Just because you are referred to someone, doesn't mean they're the best fit for you. Over this period of time, I've learned that if a person's way of practicing doesn't align with my beliefs that it's not a reason to stop going to therapy in totality. One must simply try someone else.

For those of you who don't know what any of these counselors are, I'd like to explain them to you. My grief counselors were individuals who were put in place to strictly talk to me about grieving the loss of my son. My therapists help me navigate through all of my life journeys and past traumas. Finally, my psychiatrists treat my mental health.

When I lost my son, each of these individuals played a vital role when it came to different avenues of my life that I needed assistance with. I had to work on each of those aspects of my life.

My grief counselor focused on giving me positive and healthy ways to grieve Nigel's death. I was connected with other mothers who lost their sons to suicide. I attended group sessions to meet with other parents who lost their kids to suicide as well. Grief counseling was great when it came to me focusing on healing from my son's death.

Now, when it comes to my regular therapist, oh my God. Let's address my relationship with my boyfriend. Let's address my relationships with my family members. Let's address my childhood trauma. Let us just get it all together.

Lastly, when it came to my psychiatrist, I went to see them to obtain a plan of care. The psychiatrist had to put together a plan that would get my brain functioning the way a brain is actually supposed to function. So, I don't feel bad and neither am I ashamed to admit that I've actually had to see this many people to keep me intact. At the end of the day, my baby is gone, but I still have to live.

If I'm going to live, I may as well use the time that God is allowing me—to live a life with a healthy mind. Because these people help me, I'm able to hold down a 4.0 Grade Point Average (GPA) in school. I'm able to focus on getting things done in honor of my son. I'm able to focus on doing what I have to do to take care of my family.

I hate the stigma that says "Black people don't go to therapy" because Black people need to go to therapy. I feel like I should say that again. BLACK PEOPLE NEED TO GO TO THERAPY.

You know what, I'm not gonna just make it about us…PEOPLE NEED TO GO TO THERAPY. When your mental health is not functioning at its optimal level, there is nothing wrong with you seeking treatment. Let me take y'all to church for a second.

If bitches don't like the fact that they don't have ass, what do they do? They go buy a new ass! If we don't like the fact that our stomach is not functioning the way that we want it to function or look the way we want it to look, what do we do? We do something about that stomach. If a person is not satisfied with the way their nose looks, what do they do? They go get a new nose. So, if you can do this to the parts of your body that you feel aren't working or looking the way that you want them to, why won't you have the same energy when it comes to your brain? I will never understand.

Your mind tells the rest of your body what to do. If your mind ain't right, how the hell the rest of your body gonna be right?

FROM TRAGEDY TO TRIUMPH

Ultimately, I knew that Nigel was a gift that God sent me, and everything happened the way that it happened because that's how God wanted it to happen. I'm not in the business of questioning it anymore. In addition to my questioning, you see that I've been depressed for four years, I've blamed myself, I've blamed everyone else, and I've given it all of the negative attention that I had left in me. I pray that each person's mind may be opened before they read and process the next paragraph.

My child's death was a gut-wrenching tragedy, but it was also a blessing. I say this because my child sacrificed his life for a world of people! If that ain't Jesus like, then I don't know what is. My baby's death is a blessing to a lot of people. It's crazy, but I remember me saying, I'm about to show y'all how to turn a tragedy into triumph. I posted those words about six months after Nigel's death. God forgive little ol' me for believing that I gave birth to an angel! I'm sorry but that's just how I feel. I feel as if God put an angel in my womb to bring into this world, and when He was ready to receive him back, He wanted me to use this message that this angel left upon us to put out into the world. I can't be anything else other than grateful for that.

Do you know how many children commit suicide and people don't know them? I gave birth to a chosen child. Although his death is what made him chosen, I still believe that I birthed a chosen child. I can't be sad about that anymore; my MOST PRAISED CHAMPION did what he was set out to do in this world.

I can only accept it for what it is. I know it may sound or seem weird to people because in others mind lies, but she lost her child. Yes, I lost my child, but I gained my life. Birthing Nigel gave me a purpose. Losing him gave me even more purpose because it set me up to help more people. I lost one child and gained an entire world full of people who need love and help. This is why I try to walk differently, but I am still human and imperfect.

There are times where I will revert back to the old me, quick—into my flesh. But for the most part, I try to remain humble and live in my truths. I know that those are the only things that are going to keep me grounded and where I need to be. My Nigel was a blessing in disguise, but he died a tragic fate. When I close my eyes sometimes, I still see his little lifeless eyes and it eats my soul to the core and makes my heart hurt so bad. But in that same light, I have to be grateful that God lended our son to me for 15 years.

After four years, I have finally gotten rid of all of his belongings. Well, not all because I still have to hold on to some memories. I have his hoodie with the heat pressed rainbow that you all see, and his Tommy Hilfiger bath robe and pants that he loved to wear. My house is still covered with pictures of Nigel everywhere to the point that it's somewhat overwhelming at times. I know that the day is going to come where I have to remove some things so that his face won't be in every corner that I look in. I know that it'll only come when I heal more. As of now, I am not in a rush. I will feel what I feel.

As a parent, there is a subconscious fear of something happening to your child. Losing my son has made me fearless. When and if that time comes that something tragic happens to your child(ren)or you have to bury your child, your worst fear has come true. Once you experience and live through your worst fear anything else feels like a breeze. It makes you think, damn, I've made it through my worst fear. That doesn't mean that I don't have simple fears such as being afraid of heights. It means that I don't fear life's obstacles, roadblocks, or disappointments.

The fear of disappointing the next person has been something that I've dealt with since a child. I have always been a people pleaser, but I don't care to please anyone anymore. It no longer serves a purpose in my life. The boundaries that I have set are hard for people to understand because they are used to havin' their way with me.

In this phase of my life, I feel like I'm standing my ground. I can say what I mean and mean what I say when it comes to people. I have always struggled with this. There was a time where I may have told a person no, then they'd do a little more convincing to the point where I'd eventually change my answer to yes.

When you have a taste of who you are, people grow afraid. Oftentimes, they want you where they can suck the life out of you. I was blinded by the most powerful powers that I possessed—knowing who I was and my uniqueness and light that I offer the world. People try their hardest to put me in a box.

People tend to want to put outspoken or loud people in a box. Instead of accepting you for who you are, people tend to tone you down, limit your thoughts, or dim your light. Nigel felt as if he was put in a box. Being put in a box is like me telling someone my favorite color is green and them trying to explain why my favorite color should be blue. Damnit, just accept what I like and allow me to like what I like. Letting someone control your thoughts and feelings or having a say so over your decisions is all a part of letting someone put you in a box.

Before I lost Nigel, it was my nature to cover up or hide things that the next person felt was wrong. It was human nature not doing something that made you happy because the next person felt that it was embarrassing. But guess what? Because of my son's death, I don't fear being me anymore. I don't fear society telling me what they think of my actions. The world can no longer project any feelings on me, so I'm not going anywhere near the box for someone to push me inside of it.

I have realized that the only person that I can allow to dim my light is myself. I will no longer give anyone else the authority to bring darkness upon me. If I ever make a wrong decision in this lifetime, I have faith knowing that God will teach me the lesson(s) and correct me.

I vow to be unapologetic about who I am and who I'm becoming. Yet, I'm wise enough to know that the person who's telling you all this story will not be the same person five years from now. We as human beings tend to think that because my opinion does not match their opinion, my opinion matters more. It really doesn't. Truth be told, they are all JUST OPINIONS. It doesn't make either party right or wrong, but it makes us different. That's it. Embrace your differences! I truly wish that people would stop being so judgmental of things that they don't know, feel or understand. Nigel was truly a pure soul.

I'm not sure what all the future holds for me, but I do know a few things for sure, I will make sure that The Nigel Shelby Foundation, flourishes and helps as many people as God allows. I also know that because of that sunshine that glistened from his smile, the warmth that filled his heart, the joy that he brought to a room, the laughter he gave when telling a joke, because of the kindness and love that he showed, there will always be…A NEED FOR NIGEL.

The end

SPECIAL THANKS

I would like to thank each and every one of you for your love and support for Nigel and I. This journey has been long, hard, not to mention draining, and without your support and encouragement, I wouldn't have made it this far.

-Camika

www.ingramcontent.com/pod-product-compliance
Lightning Source LLC
Chambersburg PA
CBHW060537130626
46553CB00002B/795